HARDY TREES
TREES
and
SHRUBS

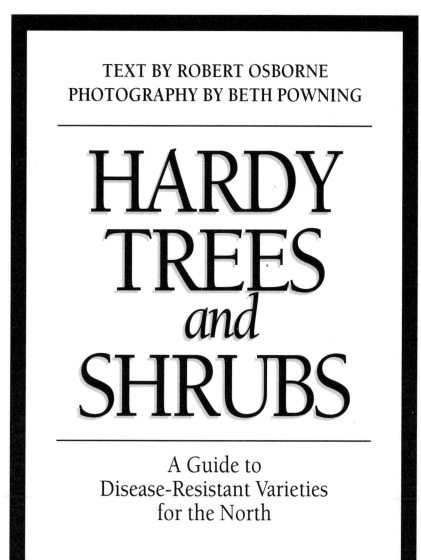

TEXT BY ROBERT OSBORNE
PHOTOGRAPHY BY BETH POWNING

HARDY TREES *and* SHRUBS

A Guide to
Disease-Resistant Varieties
for the North

Canadian Cataloguing in Publication Data

Osborne, Robert
Hardy trees and shrubs: a guide to disease-
resistant varieties for the north

Includes index.
ISBN 1-55013-633-X (cloth)
ISBN 1-55013-760-3 (paper)

1. Trees.   2. Shrubs.   3. Trees – Disease and pest
resistance.   4. Shrubs – Disease and pest resistance.
5. Organic gardening.   I. Powning, Beth.
II. Title.

SB435.072 1996   635.9'77   C94-932723-9

The publisher gratefully acknowledges the
assistance of the Canada Council and the
Ontario Arts Council.

Design: Jean Lightfoot Peters
Electronic Layout: Heidi Palfrey

Printed and bound in Canada

Key Porter Books Limited
70 The Esplanade
Toronto, Ontario
Canada M5E 1R2

96 97 98 99 5 4 3 2 1

Occasionally a conifer will form a congested mass of growth called a witch's broom. I found a dying witch's broom hanging from a branch of a jack pine growing in a cemetery not far from our home. I grafted cuttings and several grew. The following year the witch's broom died, as did my father, who was buried in that same cemetery. The soil that now accepts my father has given me unique kernels of growth that nourish themselves in my garden's soil.

My father showed me the plants in the woods and fields and taught me the value of words. I owe this book to him.

Bob Osborne

To my father and mother, Wendell and Alison Davis, with love.

Beth Powning

Contents

INTRODUCTION / ix

1. NURTURING / 1

   Site / 1
   Soil / 3
   •Soil Texture / 5
   •The Nutrient Cycle / 7
   •The Nitrogen Cycle / 8
   •Soil Supplements / 10
   Water / 12
   Cultivation and Weed Control / 13
   Planting / 14
   Pruning / 17
   •Pruning Shrubs / 19
   •Pruning Deciduous Trees / 22
   •Pruning Evergreens / 25
   •Root Pruning / 26
   •The Tools / 27
   Diseases and Insects / 28
   •Diseases and Recipes to Control Them / 31
   •Insects and Recipes to Control Them / 33

2. DECIDUOUS TREES / 36

3. CONIFERS / 48

4. FLOWERING SHRUBS / 66

5. BROADLEAF EVERGREENS / 80

   APPENDIX OF HARDY SPECIES / 86

   INDEX / 109

Introduction

AS I GAZE UPON THE WINTRY BONES OF A DISTANT GNARLED TREE, A JAY is startled from its perch, its cry the only sound to touch the silence. The air is cold, the spring is but a memory, a hope. We gardeners of the north know well the long and anxious wait for the wakening of life. We must endure the splitting of the trunks and freezing of the buds; we know the murder done by frost and snow.

It is the wait that makes the spring's warm touch so sweet. Those whose winter is a month of cold, or maybe two, can never feel how bright the sun's long rays can be. We leap into our gardens as though possessed, and revel in the blossom and the fruit.

For those of us driven to garden in the north, the dreams of fragrant blooms on arching boughs are often shattered by the realities of our winters. How often have you spared no expense to make your tree a paragon of health only to find it a blackened skeleton when spring arrived? I know of what I speak, for my plants have often suffered winter's crystal fangs. In my search for hardy trees and shrubs, I have cast aside many that did not have the fortitude necessary to survive, but there have been many successes as well. By knowing which varieties to plant, your gardening efforts are more likely to be rewarded by the scent of newly opened flowers than the sight of shriveled buds.

One of the most critical decisions you make when planning a garden is the variety of plant you grow. If the variety is not hardy, the task of keeping your plant alive and healthy will be daunting indeed. Thousands of varieties are sold by countless nurseries, garden centers and mail-order houses. Trying to sort through the information, misinformation and hype to discover which varieties are most suitable is fascinating to some, frustrating for most.

As if the endless struggle against winter is not enough, you must find ways to protect your trees and shrubs against the ravages of insects and disease. Though there are many paths you can follow to accomplish this task, it seems to me the most logical starting point is to choose plants that have a natural resistance to pests. Such plants will require less care and should not need to be "protected" by insecticides and fungicides, materials whose use can cause disruptions in the normal functioning of soil life, and whose misuse can contaminate water, air, soil and food.

Accepting the limitations of a northern garden and setting limits on how you grow your garden can provide an opportunity to expand your expertise and thereby enhance your enjoyment of your garden. The search for hardy trees and shrubs may lead to the discovery of fascinating new plants. If you wish to grow plants without insecticides, it is in your interest to learn more about the life cycles of insects and the plants that resist their attacks. If you do not want to use fungicides, you should learn more about the conditions that foster fungal growth. Forgoing herbicides entails learning more about those plants that compete with your trees and shrubs. Books will help immensely in this learning process, but nothing will teach you more than keen observation. You can often learn more about the lives of insects by quietly watching their activities on a shrub than by reading about them. It is important to observe with objectivity. Too often we label animals and plants "good" or "bad." They, just as we, are all part of a vast, connected life system and are no more or less important than any other part. What you observe may surprise and, I hope, fascinate you.

The sights, smells, touches, tastes and sounds are ample rewards for the work a garden entails, but they are only the tangible results. The knowledge you gain by observing and influencing the intricate ebb and flow of life in your garden will increase your understanding of nature's cycles. As a keen observer, you cannot help but gain a better appreciation and respect for the importance of diversity in the natural world. To glimpse a tiny portion of its complexity is to stand at the edge of the universe. The final reward of gardening is a sense of humility, peace and ceaseless awe.

If the infinity of it all overwhelms you, do not worry. Simply grab a shovel and begin.

The Earth harbors an array of trees and shrubs that is tremendously diverse, but you live on a particular patch of that Earth, with a unique climate, geology and topography. The trees and shrubs that you grow will be subject to the conditions in your garden.

Cold winter temperatures limit the number of different plants you can grow. The farther north your garden, the more you are limited. This book is an attempt to guide your selections toward trees and shrubs that are reliable performers in many northern gardens. When their growing needs are met, these plants are generally free of disease and insect problems. They have been chosen with a bias toward plants that are native to the colder sections of North America. Plants that have grown in your area for centuries have usually developed resistances to the environmental stresses, diseases and insects that occur where you live, making it more likely they will prosper in your garden. A great number of trees and shrubs used in the northern landscape are introductions from many areas of the world, and some of them have proven to be valuable additions, providing new colors, textures and possibilities in garden plantings.

Trees and shrubs reproduce by seed, but many of the plants in our gardens exist because of the art of propagation. The horticultural world contains a menagerie of seedlings, thought unique enough to save by rooting cuttings or grafting pieces of the original plant. This represents for the gardener a living museum, works of nature's art. These museum pieces can be had by anyone with some coin of the realm or the talents of a plantsman. A work of art in a museum gathers dust, but the art growing in our garden is, in a very real sense, the same living plant that was found decades or centuries ago and kept youthful by skillful hands wielding sharp knives.

For those unfamiliar with the Latin names used in horticulture, a bit of explanation may help. Plants are divided into groups, determined primarily by the form of their flowers and fruit. The entire plant world is called the plant kingdom. This kingdom is further divided into phyllums, orders, families, genuses and species. Plants of a species generally cannot reproduce with plants outside their species. Groups of similar species are genuses. Take, for example, the Norway spruce. This conifer's Latin name is *Picea Abies*. Its species name is *Abies*, and it belongs to the genus *Picea*, which includes all the spruces.

A species, such as the Norway spruce, propagates by seed. Within the species, every individual seedling is genetically unique. If a seedling is chosen to be asexually propagated by grafting or cuttings, its characteristics will be reproduced identically, and it becomes a horticultural "clone," more often called a "variety." A popular form of the Norway spruce is the nest spruce. Its Latin name is *Picea Abies* 'Nidiformis'. The Latin name Nidiformis signifies that this clone (or variety) has a nest-like (nidi) form (formis). The clone name, which always appears in single quotes, identifies plants that are identical to this form. Example: A form of spruce commonly called 'nest spruce'. Its Latin name is:

Picea	*Abies*	'Nidiformis'
Genus: Spruce	Species: Norway	Clone: Nest-like form

This book will deal with species of trees and shrubs and with clones (or varieties) within those species. Although technically a variety can include a group of similar plants, for our purposes we will use the terms "clone" and "variety" interchangeably. Occasionally you will see the symbol "×" used in a Latin name, such as *Magnolia* × *Loebneri* 'Merrill'. This symbol indicates that the variety, in this case 'Merrill', is a hybrid between different species.

Nurturing

UNDERSTANDING THE PROCESS OF GROWTH HELPS YOU DETERMINE courses of action or inaction that will enable you to grow trees and shrubs to their potential.

SITE

Swollen from early spring rains, a seed splits its shell. Inside are two halves.

One of the halves grows toward the center of the Earth. The cells, absorbing water as they reproduce, expand toward the path of least resistance. In this way, roots work their way down worm holes, among stones and through torn leaves. The root's outer cells allow certain substances to pass through them. Molecules, some simple, some very complex, are pulled through cell walls toward a network of pathways that push this carefully filtered beverage upward.

The seed's other half forms a system of stems and leaves, a finely tuned antenna for capturing the sun's rays. The leaves align themselves toward the sun, changing their position with the Earth's rotation in a daily progression from east to west. By a process we only partially understand, specialized tissues absorb sunlight and use the sun's energy to transform the substances drawn by the roots, in combination with air that the leaves absorb, into food. Specialized tubes of connected cells transfer this food to areas where growth is occurring in the plant. Here the energy trapped within the food is released. The result is growth.

Although plants grow upward toward the sun and delve downward into the earth, left to themselves they cannot leave their site and will grow only as well as the soil will allow. As we garden, we move plants about; the sites we choose will determine how well they grow.

Each garden is unique. Understanding your garden's particular site is critical in determining which plants you can grow successfully. Knowing your site can also help you to alter its conditions to allow you to grow specific plants. Some things about your site you cannot change, such as the overall weather patterns and the general topography of your land. You can, however, create screens to deflect wind or trap heat. You can change drainage patterns. You can stimulate more activity in the soil. You can regulate soil temperatures by cultivation or through the use of mulches. There are numerous ways you can make your garden a more amenable place in which to grow plants.

Take, for example, the temperatures in your garden. Temperature plays a vital role in the life and death of plants. When you are choosing varieties to plant, be sure that your selections are hardy enough to survive in your hardiness zone (see Zone Map). Minimum temperatures are not something over which you have any control, but by siting a plant on the leeward side of an evergreen or a hedge you can make a tremendous impact on windchill. A fully dormant plant may be able to tolerate a certain low temperature, but if this temperature is accompanied by high winds, the extra chilling of the wind will have the effect of temperatures much lower than the thermometer reads. As well, the planting of windbreaks can help trap snow, a very effective insulator. With an early snow cover, temperatures just below the ground's surface will not fall very much lower than freezing. A good cover of snow may protect many of the stems as well. Often the location of snow-trapping plants or fences will mean the difference between the survival and death of a plant.

Many sites have differences in elevation or proximity to buildings. On still nights, heavier cold air collects in low areas. Plants in such areas may experience lower temperatures in winter and, even more importantly, may be frosted on spring nights when temperatures hover near freezing. A few feet in elevation may mean the difference between a spectacular display of floral extravagance and a discouraging scene of black, wilted petals. Planting near buildings makes use of heat escaping from the building. Even unheated buildings act as heat traps, releasing the trapped heat at night. This same heat can be a danger, however. Trees and shrubs planted on the south side of a building may be stimulated into breaking dormancy earlier, making them more susceptible to early spring freezes.

Many species of trees and shrubs can be injured if they are placed where the late afternoon sun of a still winter day keeps bark warm and therefore thawed. At sunset, its warming rays are replaced by frigid temperatures. The nearly instant freezing quickly causes the bark to contract, and the result is a vertical split in the trunk that precisely marks the direction of the sun's disappearance, giving "southwest injury" its name. This same effect also damages the leaves of evergreen shrubs such

Placing shrubs on the leeward side of a structure such as a wall creates eddies in the wind patterns that cause snow to drop and accumulate. This extra snow acts as an insulated blanket, protecting the plant against low temperatures.

as rhododendrons, turning their dark green leaves into brown curled wafers. Species that cannot tolerate these conditions are best sited facing east and protected from the rays of the afternoon sun. If this is not possible, give them some shading from the afternoon sun.

Knowing what we can and cannot change in our gardens is critical to success. You cannot change the overall wind pattern on your hill, but by putting protective plants in certain spots you can create pockets where you can grow species too tender for more exposed sites. You cannot force more rain out of the clouds above you, but you can create humus-rich soils that capture water and keep it near the soil's surface where plants can use it. You cannot change the date of the first and last frosts, but by selecting species and varieties that are adapted to your seasons, you can have the fruits and flowers that are the rewards of gardening.

Study your garden, your site. Know the directions of the wind, the path of the sun, the character of the soil, the length of the seasons, the winter temperatures. The more you involve yourself in the details of your garden the easier it will be to make decisions about it. Never forget that you have the most notable affect on your garden. You dig, you cultivate, you prune, you fertilize, you affect the garden with the materials you bring into it, the materials you move within it, and the materials you remove from it. Respect your capacity to change the garden. Treading lightly usually serves both garden and gardener well.

SOIL

The flower's sweet perfume has its origins among the corpses of the soil. Its fragile blossom has been drawn from a brew of eye of root, toe of log, wing of gnat and tongue of fog. Hidden from our eyes lies a world where one-celled bacteria slowly dissolve the woody tissue of leaves, where tender fallen petals are devoured by the rasping mouths of snails, where voracious larvae follow lightless worm tunnels toward unsuspecting gnats feeding on tiny fungi. In crevices between grains of sand and in the hollow cores of branches long ago covered by the ceaseless rain of leaves and twigs, beetles, fattened on ant eggs and hapless mites, leave their castings. Water, following its downward course through stone and litter, dissolves such dungs, forming liquids that the probing roots of plants absorb. Each species of plant selects from this "soup" the necessary simple and complex molecules in the quantities

Placing shrubs in groups or on the leeward side of larger trees helps to trap insulating snow.

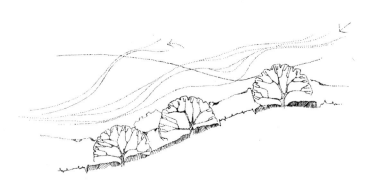

Underneath the soil's surface is a world, populated by bacteria, fungi, plants and animals competing for food and space, that is as complex and important as the world above it.

specific to its requirements. As the leaves turn toward the sun, adjusting continuously to capture its most intense rays, this mixture we call sap, drawn from the soil below, is transformed into the sugars that contain energy for growth.

We gardeners tread upon the soil every day, yet understand very little about the complex events that are constantly unfolding within it.

Walk into your garden. Pick a spot. Dig a hole, but this time don't use any tools. Try to dig a hole large enough for a plant with your hands. If you can't, grab a handy stick or suitably shaped rock. Now try. In most gardens this will be a more daunting task than you may imagine.

I do this fairly often, not because I have an exceptional affinity for burrowing animals, but because I can learn more about the soil this way than any number of books can teach me. Although I cannot delve through the soil with the finesse of a root tip, I can experience on an intimate level the composition, the density, the feel of the soil. I can observe a small part of the life inhabiting the soil. I can smell the soil. I can taste it.

The soil is a subject that needs to be understood. Humanity has quickly (nearly instantly, if you are a planet) eroded away the vital living skin of Earth. Our farming and forestry practices have consumed its fragile skin as the leaf miner skeletonizes its host. Although there are now many more people needing to be fed, the best soils are gone. We have built our cities on the finest, flattest land. The best soil remaining is exhausted from overuse and polluted with a host of materials. It is an alarming story. We need to acquire the gardener's soft steps, for if we do not cherish the soil from which our food comes, we will eventually perish.

Soil Texture

The processes of glaciation, water and wind erosion, freezing and chemical action by water and plants continuously break down the surface rocks of the Earth and move these pieces about its surface. The soil in your garden is a unique slice of that surface. The types of rock from which it is derived, the size of the particles of which it is composed and the plants that have grown on it will determine the nature of your soil and its possibilities. Not all soils are created equal.

Most soils are combinations of four basic components. These are sand, silt, clay and humus. Sand is created by the gradual pulverization of silica, the most common mineral on Earth. When silica breaks apart, it forms irregular pieces that become more rounded as they are reduced in size. Beach sand is an example of a silica sand. The particles are small and rounded and will not stick together when dry. Silt is composed of extremely fine particles that are brought together by water or wind erosion. Silts will stick together but are easily broken apart. Soils with a large silt component are often found along rivers and in their deltas. Some soils, called loess soils, are almost totally composed of silts brought in by wind. Clays are derived from rocks composed of generally insoluble compounds that are weathered down into flat plate-like particles that adhere closely to one another. When water is added, the plates slip sideways, creating the typical elastic feel of clay. It is this property that the potter utilizes to make pots. Humus is the remains of plant life that have decomposed to a stage that is relatively stable. It is usually a dark brown or black material in the soil.

You may remember from your science lessons that things have positive or negative electrical charges. Most of us have rubbed a balloon in our hair and stuck it on a wall. This is an example of the attraction between the negatively charged balloon and the positively charged wall. It is also true that two positively charged items will repel each other, as will two negatively charged items. These simple principles affect the texture and, ultimately, the fertility of your soil.

The particles of clay and humus in the soil have negative charges. Positively charged elements such as calcium, magnesium, potassium and sodium are attracted to the clay and humus particles and bond to them. When there is an abundance of these positively charged elements attaching themselves to the clay and humus, the clay and humus particles lose their negative charges and combine to form small lumps. In such a soil the texture is crumbly. If you squeeze such a soil it will compress together but will easily shatter when dropped. This soil will hold water well, but has pore spaces between the clay–humus balls to allow water and air to penetrate. Such a soil has an ideal texture for plant growth.

Most northern gardeners live where rain is abundant and temperatures are cool. As the water moves down through the soil, it carries away minerals that are soluble. These include the positively charged elements, most importantly calcium and magnesium. As water combines with these elements, they are removed from the surfaces of the clay and humus particles. The clay and humus particles become more negatively charged and begin to repel one another. When this happens, the crumbly texture of the soil changes. In soils where there is little clay, the humus is gradually carried down through the particles of sand until it lies well below the zone used by most plant roots, leaving the upper soil less able to hold nutrients and water, and therefore less fertile and drier. In soils that are largely clay, the clay particles have a tendency to push apart from one another, and within these soils the clay will distribute itself evenly throughout the soil, inhibiting the movement of water and air.

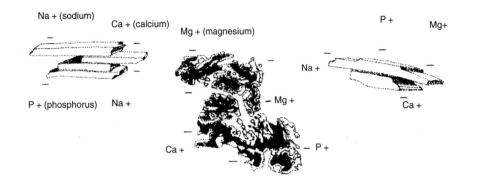

Particles of clay and humus are negatively charged and repel each other. Sufficient supplies of positively charged elements such as magnesium and calcium, which are attracted to the clay and humus, neutralize these particles, drawing them together into small clay–humus clumps that give such soils a loose, loamy texture.

The surface of such a soil during a rain will form sheets of clay particles that crack when dry.

In order to create or preserve proper soil texture, you must find ways to be sure that enough of the positively charged elements are present to create the bond between clay and humus that is essential for good texture. The simplest and least expensive method to maintain this bond in most gardens is by adding ground limestone. When you add lime to your soil, water begins to dissolve the small particles, freeing calcium and magnesium to bond to the clay and humus particles. Regular light applications of lime will guarantee a steady supply of positively charged elements. In this way you can help maintain a loose and crumbly texture in your soil. Not all soils will need lime. In order to determine if you need limestone, and if so, how much, you should have your soil tested.

A soil test will measure the pH (potential hydrogen) of your soil. The pH scale runs from 0 to 14, 0 being most acidic, 14 being most alkaline and 7 being neutral. As a general rule, most soils in the colder and damper areas of the world are acidic. In soils that contain limestone there may be enough available calcium to keep the pH higher. In wet boggy soils pH levels may dip as low as 4, which is very acidic. A soil test should tell you if you need lime and, if so, how much lime will bring your soil into the range best suited to the plants you want to grow. Most departments of agriculture do soil tests for the public, but there are also private businesses that specialize in such tests. Although most trees and shrubs prefer a range of 6 to 7, some crops such as rhododendrons and azaleas need a more acidic soil. Be sure to check the optimum range for each of your trees and shrubs and adjust your soil accordingly.

If you garden in a naturally acidic soil, it is advisable to maintain the proper pH level by applying light applications of lime every year or two. If you wait until the pH drops to lower levels you will sacrifice growth during the time it takes for the lime to dissolve and bring the pH back to the desired level.

If you live in a dry climate, particularly a warm, dry climate, your approach to the soil must be different. In such climates, there is more evaporation of water and the movement of water in soils tends to be upward. In these soils, the soluble elements such as calcium and magnesium are carried to the surface where they accumulate as salts. If you have grown houseplants, you have probably noticed a white powder developing on the pot rim and the surface of the soil. In the warm, dry air of the house, evaporation is carrying water and the dissolved salts upward. When they reach the surface, they can go no further and they accumulate as a white powder.

The accumulation of these salts causes dry soils to become alkaline. Some trees and shrubs have adapted to alkaline conditions and these should be used in alkaline soils. However, most trees and shrubs have a difficult time growing in alkaline soil because the excess salts draw water away from the plant, burning the tissues. Alkaline soils can be adjusted by adding acidic materials such as sulfur to the soil. Highly alkaline soils are less common in northern areas and do not concern most cold-climate gardeners.

To a great degree the texture of your soil will be governed by the amount of clay, sand, silt and humus it contains. It is generally not feasible to import large quantities of sand into a clay soil or clay into a sandy soil. If you are working with a soil that contains no clay, it is possible to buy high-quality clays, such as Bentonite, which will help to create the clay-humus complex so important for good soil texture, but most soil contains enough clay so that this is not necessary.

Your garden has its own mixture of clay, sand, silt and humus, and by altering the acidity levels of your soil, you can affect its texture. But there is another important method of altering your soil's texture and, ultimately, its fertility. This is the addition of organic matter. Organic matter, in combination with lime in acidic soils, will help to aerate heavy clay soils and will help sandy soils better hold water and nutrients. Organic matter is much more, however. It forms the key ingredient in a cycle of life and death that feeds your trees and shrubs.

The Nutrient Cycle

As a gardener, you endeavor to remove or reduce factors that limit a plant's potential for growth. You ensure your plants have adequate sunlight and space. You try to protect your plants from injurious temperatures. You provide them with adequate water. You must also ensure they have a soil that will provide them with all the nutrients necessary for optimum growth. Just as a chain is only as strong as its weakest link, a plant's ability to grow can be constrained by an inadequate supply of a single nutrient. Creating and maintaining soils that contain all the essential elements for plant growth is one of the most challenging tasks you face. Understanding how plants feed will help you to accomplish this task.

Plants obtain nutrients from the air, from the dissolving particles of rock and from the decaying remains of other plants and animals in the soil.

The greatest percentage of a plant's structure is carbon, but plants are unable to take carbon directly from the remains of other plants. They absorb their carbon from the atmosphere. Small pores called stomata, which are located on the surface of leaves, draw in carbon dioxide from the air. Water, which is composed of oxygen and hydrogen, is drawn from the soil by the root system and is pumped upward into the leaves. The leaves have cells that contain chlorophyll. The crystalline structure of chlorophyll becomes "excited" when sunlight strikes it. Energy from the sunlight is absorbed and used by the chlorophyll to break apart the carbon dioxide and water to create sugars in a process called photosynthesis. Oxygen is the by-product of this reaction and it is released back into the atmosphere through the stomata. This is why plants are called oxygen pumps and why we depend on them for our very existence. The molecular bonds that hold sugars together contain the energy absorbed during photosynthesis. Where growth is occurring in the plant, the sugars are broken down by the cells, and the energy is released to fuel the growth. In a very real sense you "feed" a plant by allowing it to have access to adequate sunlight and water. Without them, a plant cannot produce its food. If either is in short supply, a plant will not grow to its potential.

Plants use a number of minerals, which they obtain either directly from the dissolving particles of rock in the soil or from the decomposition of organic matter.

The process by which plants obtain minerals directly from the parent rock is quite startling. As you might imagine, water percolating through the soil dissolves rock particles extremely slowly, and in a plant's life this process is relatively unimportant. But the microscopic life in the soil, most importantly bacteria, indirectly creates conditions that dissolve these minerals more quickly. As these microbes feed they excrete organic acids that disintegrate the surfaces of rock particles. As minerals are released, they combine with the acids to form salts, which are readily absorbed by plants. Most fascinating of all, however, is that plants actually contribute to this activity by feeding the microbes near their roots.

Nearly 20% of the food produced by plants is transferred to the root zone, where it is injected into the soil. By making food available to the microbes in the soil, plants help to increase their populations, thereby also increasing the amount of organic acids produced. In this way, the dissolving of minerals in the area around the roots is speeded up, and the supply of these minerals increases. The type of rocks your soil contains will, in great measure, determine which minerals can be made available by this process, an important reason that soils differ widely in fertility. A sandy soil that is essentially composed of silica and little else can never be as productive as a soil derived from sedimentary rocks, which are themselves made up of particles eroded from a wide assortment of rocks. However, plants can extract minerals from the decomposing remains of plants and animals, and in this way you can change soils that have little natural fertility into productive soils.

When a plant dies, its remains contain the elements necessary to nourish another such plant. It is the process of decomposition that enables living plants to use the elements contained within dead plants. Microscopic soil life begins feeding on the sugars, starches and proteins in a dead plant as soon as it dies. The microbes use the energy in the sugars and starches for growth. Their waste products are the same substances that the plant used to create the sugars – carbon dioxide, which is released back into the air, and water, which enters the soil. Some proteins are used by the soil life for growth and reproduction while others not needed are excreted. As each species of soil life increases in population, their predators increase as well. These, in turn, are consumed by larger and more complex creatures. Soon a vast array of animals is in the soil, feeding on one another and releasing excrement that contains nutrients that dissolve in the soil water. From this brew, the plant roots can extract the vitally needed elements once contained in the dead plants.

The Nitrogen Cycle

Nitrogen has often been called the key element in plant growth. It is no more important than other elements plants need, but it cannot be obtained from the mineral soil. It is found only in the atmosphere and in the bodies of plants and animals. Plants cannot directly absorb nitrogen from the atmosphere. Although the group of plants called legumes forms an association with specialized bacteria that provide them with nitrogen in exchange for sugars from the plants, most plants derive their entire supply of nitrogen from the decay of plant and animal bodies.

Plants and animals are made up of many different materials, including proteins, which are complex molecules that contain nitrogen. Proteins are essential components of cell structures and are necessary for growth and reproduction. When bacteria, fungi, insects, worms and others feed on dead plants and animals, they separate out and break down these proteins for their own use and pass some in their

The roots of plants release sugars that feed soil microbes near them. The increased activity leads to a higher level of organic acids, released by the microbes. These acids accelerate the dissolving of soil minerals that plants need for growth.

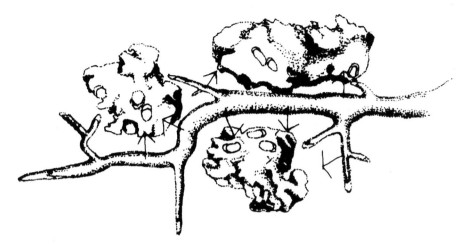

excrement. The nitrogen compounds contained in the excretions combine with water in the soil and, in this state, become available to plant roots. Nitrogen not absorbed by plants or consumed by other soil life will eventually break down into its gaseous form and return to the air.

If you want your plants to have an adequate supply of nitrogen, you must ensure that the decomposition of organic matter in the soil does not stop or slow down. A soil that is not active with dead-plant eaters will not release adequate nitrogen into the soil for optimal growth. In such soils, plants will grow slowly, and in very low-nitrogen soils plants will appear yellowed and stunted.

A natural forest or meadow replenishes its supply of organic matter by the annual addition of leaves, dead branches and the accumulated debris of the animals living in the forest or meadow. In a garden that is cultivated, the process of decomposition is speeded up, making it necessary to put organic matter in the soil on a regular basis to ensure a continuous supply of dead plant and animal matter that soil life can break down. Without replenishing the soil with dead bodies, eventually the material in the soil will have been broken down to the point that very little decomposition takes place.

The nitrogen cycle in your soil is something like a self-sustaining engine. If nitrogen is available to the bacteria, they can reproduce, and decomposition speeds up. As the bacteria multiply, excrete and die, other organisms feed on them. If there is a sufficient supply of organic matter to be broken down and there is adequate oxygen, the process generates more and more life. More life creates more death and excrement, resulting in higher concentrations of available nitrogen and other materials used by your plants. The most active soils contain tremendous populations of animals, both simple and complex. Soils with large populations of worms, insects and small mammals are dynamic soils where the nutrient cycle is in balance.

This is a delicate balance and it can be easily disrupted. For example, you can temporarily overload your soil with organic matter. Organic materials vary in their composition. Animal bodies, leaves and the softer tissues of plants decompose readily because they contain high levels of nitrogen, which the bacteria require to grow and reproduce. The woody parts of plants, such as tree trunks and branches, contain little nitrogen. They are composed of materials such as lignin, which is difficult to break down. If you incorporate a large amount of wood shavings or sawdust into your soil, you have introduced a tremendous amount of difficult-to-digest material into the soil. The bacteria populations in the soil will absorb any available nitrogen as they reproduce to feed on the wood fiber. But if nitrogen levels in the soil are low, the populations will not have enough nitrogen to multiply to the levels needed to decompose the wood fiber, and with virtually all the available nitrogen tied by the bacteria, there will be little left for your plants, and they will suffer. That is not to say wood fiber is bad. Far from it. Although there is a temporary depletion of nitrogen, bacteria will continue to break down the wood fiber. Once the initial breakdown occurs, a rapid explosion of soil life will take place, and nitrogen levels will rise to the point where there is enough to fill your plants' needs.

Soil Supplements

Every day the forest floor receives a steady rain of leaves, sticks, dead insects, spent flowers and animal droppings. Slowly the soil life breaks down the accumulated litter into food for the trees and shrubs whose roots it covers. It may take centuries of leaves and sticks and droppings to create a deep soil rich in stable humus. In your garden you can speed this process by incorporating various supplements into your soil.

Compost

Although you can add organic matter such as leaves, hay, manure, bark, sawdust or seaweed directly to your soil, it is of more immediate value to your trees and shrubs if it is composted first. Composted materials have been broken down by soil life to a stage where their further breakdown will release nutrients into the soil that plants can use. By piling organic matter and mixing it with a source of nitrogen, you can speed the breakdown of the organic matter. It is relatively simple to make good compost if you have a basic understanding of the materials you use to create it.

All organic materials break down, but some decompose faster than others. This depends to a large extent on the carbon:nitrogen ratio – the amount of carbon in the material in relation to the amount of nitrogen. Animal products such as bloodmeal, feathers, skin or fishmeal have a very high percentage of nitrogen in relation to the amount of carbon and break down very rapidly. Soft leafy materials such as grass clippings or green hay also have a fairly high percentage of nitrogen and break down relatively quickly. Materials such as bark, sawdust, wood chips and branches have a very low percentage of nitrogen and break down very slowly unless a source of nitrogen is added. Nitrogen is critical in composting because the bacteria that initiate the breakdown of organic material need nitrogen to function. When you build a compost pile you need enough nitrogen in your pile to create rapid decomposition.

To build a compost pile, begin by putting down a layer of materials such as old hay, leaves or any other organic materials that are at hand. Then sprinkle a layer of a nitrogen-rich material such as fresh manure, bloodmeal or fishmeal. Add another layer of organic material, then another sprinkling of the high-nitrogen material. Sprinkle a few shovelfuls of soil as you proceed to provide soil microbes. Light dustings of ground limestone can be layered if you want a sweet (high pH) soil. As you build the pile, water the materials so that they are damp, but not soggy. Do not build the pile higher than 5 ft. (1.5 m). Let the pile sit for several days, and then start turning it.

Turning a compost pile is essential to its success. The billions of bacteria that are at work breaking down the organic material require oxygen. If you do not turn, or otherwise introduce oxygen into the pile, decomposition will slow. As you turn the pile, clouds of steam should accompany each forkful. An active pile will produce temperatures so high that you cannot comfortably hold your hand in the pile. This

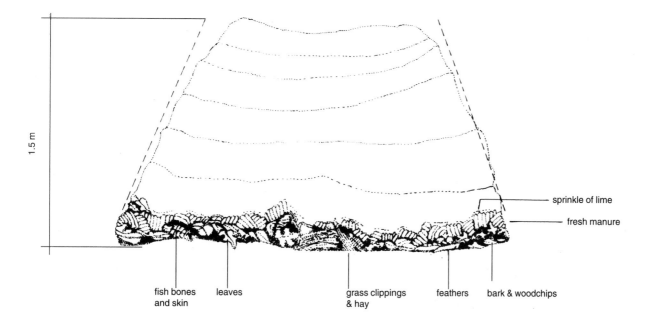

1.5 m

sprinkle of lime

fresh manure

fish bones and skin

leaves

grass clippings & hay

feathers

bark & woodchips

A compost pile is built by layering organic matter such as leaves, hay or wood fiber with nitrogen-rich materials such as manure or animal by-products. The pile is kept moist and turned frequently to keep oxygen levels high. With the proper levels of nitrogen, water and oxygen, bacteria quickly break down the organic matter into a form whose further breakdown will provide a long-term source of food for plants.

is the heat produced by the countless bodies of bacteria and other soil microbes. If the pile is hot, you know that it contains enough nitrogen to make a good compost. If there is very little heat, you need to add more nitrogen-rich materials. Turning your pile frequently is one of the keys to making compost quickly. If the carbon:nitrogen ratio is correct and you turn the pile frequently, your compost can be ready to use in as soon as four to six weeks.

You will notice the pile shrinking quite rapidly in height. As the microbes digest the fibers of organic matter, they break down the carbon molecules of the plants to get the energy contained in them. The waste products of this breakdown are water and carbon dioxide. The carbon dioxide is a gas and returns to the atmosphere — much of your compost pile literally turns into air!

When turning no longer produces much heat and the texture of the compost is fine and soil-like, the compost is finished. Now the nitrogen and other elements are held in a stable material that will slowly break down in your soil, releasing elements your trees and shrubs can absorb. This material is rich in nutrients, including trace elements and other materials needed by plants in small quantities. Compost can be spread on plants with no fear of burning delicate tissues. If the compost is well made, the heat of decomposition has also destroyed weed seeds and any diseases that were present in the organic matter. In short, it is as fine a fertilizer as you could want.

Nitrogen Catalysts

You may need a source of extra nitrogen to act as a catalyst to stimulate soil activity. Soluble forms of nitrogen such as ammonium nitrate, calcium nitrate or urea, commonly sold in commercial fertilizer preparations, can provide instantly available nitrogen, but these fertilizers are quite acidic and in high concentrations can destroy many soil organisms, including some that may associate with plant roots and aid them in the uptake of nutrients. The dissolved fertilizer also moves quickly down through the soil. Most of the nitrogen ends up below the plant roots, eventually finding its way into the water systems, where it severely disrupts the normal nutrient levels of rivers and lakes.

One source of nitrogen is animal products, such as bloodmeal, fishmeal, crabmeal and meatmeal. Other sources are high-protein plant products, such as cottonseed meal, linseed meal, soybean meal and alfalfa leaves. Rather than being directly soluble, they are a nitrogen-rich food for many soil organisms that can be directly incorporated into the soil to promote an explosion in soil life. These are stable and long-lasting sources of nitrogen which will indirectly feed your plants through the activities of soil life.

Green Manures

Another method of providing nutrients to your soil is through the use of green manure crops. These are plants that are seeded in open ground and that will later be incorporated into the soil to provide organic matter. Any plants can be used as green manure, but several bear singling out. Buckwheat is particularly useful in a new garden. This broad-leaved plant creates a dense shade that effectively kills many perennial weeds such as couchgrass. It should be tilled or plowed down just as it begins flowering. Annual and perennial rye grasses are used as well. Annual rye grass will die during the winter, adding organic matter and acting as a cover during winter. Perennial rye is of great value because its roots release substances that inhibit the growth of some grasses, including couchgrass. Perhaps most valuable are the legumes, plants that associate with certain soil bacteria that can fix nitrogen from the air. Crops such as alfalfa, clover, bird's foot trefoil, peas and beans can be sown and later incorporated into the soil, either at the end of the year or in early spring. This will release a good deal of nitrogen into the soil. Although more valuable for newly established garden plots, green manures can be used in established gardens. They are an inexpensive way to add organic matter and increase the nutritional potential of your soil.

WATER

All life forms on Earth are shaped vessels of water held together by connected strands of molecules. The plant, anchored in the soil, must maintain the integrity of its vessel by absorbing water from the soil immediately surrounding its roots. If water becomes unavailable, the plant suffers stress; if water remains unavailable to the roots, the plant's tissues collapse and die. It is essential that your garden's soil be able to hold water.

If you pour water through sand or rocks, only a thin film of water will remain around each piece of sand or rock. Heat will quickly evaporate this water into the air. If you add organic matter to the sand or rocks, you change the capacity of this mixture to hold water. Organic matter, such as compost, manure, dead leaves or bark, absorbs water into its cell spaces much like a sponge holds water in its air pockets. If you carefully dig in the root system of a plant, you can observe the tiny root hairs that grow in and around bits of leaf and stem and other organic matter in the soil. The root hairs seek out the water that is held there.

No plant can live without water, yet water can also kill plants. Soils contain air spaces through which water percolates downward. When the water is prevented from moving, the air spaces remain filled with water and oxygen becomes unavailable to the roots. While some plants have mechanisms to use these low oxygen levels, most garden plants will be injured or killed by such conditions. The roots need oxygen as much as they need water.

If your soil does not drain water away quickly, you must provide drainage. This can be difficult if your topsoil is underlain with an impervious layer of clay. You may need to install drainage pipes below the root zone to carry away excess water. Slow-draining clay soils can often be helped by the addition of lime. The lime helps form clay–humus particles with air spaces between them. Organic matter such as coarse shredded bark or compost can provide more air spaces as well. A combination of these methods can usually create a better aerated soil for your trees and shrubs.

CULTIVATION AND WEED CONTROL

Why do we cultivate soil? You may answer, "To kill weeds," and certainly cultivation is the main mechanical method of killing weeds. By reducing the competition for water, space and nutrients, your plants can have the major share of these three essentials. But cultivation does far more than this.

As we've discussed, your soil contains humus, the bulk of which is the remains of plants. Some of this humus may take centuries to break down, but a good portion of it will decompose within five or ten years. If the soil is left undisturbed, this process will take longer than if you stir the soil. When you stir the soil, you increase the amount of oxygen in it. With more oxygen, the microscopic soil life will eat and reproduce more quickly. For the same reason that turning your compost pile hastens decomposition in the pile, cultivation hastens decomposition in your soil.

If decomposition is speeded up in your soil, nutrients are released more quickly to be absorbed by probing plant roots. Cultivation, therefore, increases the amount of nutrients available to your plants. By the same token, the more you cultivate, the more organic matter is consumed and the more you will need to replace in the soil.

Cultivation is used to eliminate plants that compete with your trees and shrubs for space, light, water and nutrients. The most common tools for garden cultivation are the several styles of hoes and forks that are available. Powered cultivators such as rototillers, small and large, can also be used. Cultivation tears weeds from the soil and leaves them on the surface, where they dry out and die. The best time to cultivate is on a cool morning when you are expecting a warm, dry afternoon. The cool morning makes for comfortable working conditions and by nightfall your weeds should be dead. You can remove them for aesthetic reasons, but remember that you are taking away valuable organic matter. Left on the soil's surface, they will soon disappear as they dry and decompose. If you prefer to remove them, be sure to put them in a compost pile. When cultivating with a hoe, still the most useful weeding tool ever invented, hold it nearly vertical, taking thin slices of soil. Work by pulling unhoed ground toward you in a pattern from left to right or vice versa as you move forward. A steady rhythm in hoeing will allow you to work for long periods without tiring. Forks such as the potato fork are very useful, particularly when you want to pull up long-rooted perennial weeds such as couchgrass or vetch.

Although cultivation aerates soil and kills weeds, an alternative is mulch gardening. In a mulched garden, the surface of the soil is covered by thin layers of organic material each year, much like the forest covers its soil with a yearly layer of leaves. By layering in this manner, you create an upper layer that acts to break the impact of raindrops and to slow water flow, preventing crusting of the soil and erosion. Under the upper layers, where the older mulch meets the soil, is an ideal habitat for soil life. Here, protected from the drying of wind and sun, worms can burrow, distributing their valuable castings through the soil, insects can carry on their activities without being as easily consumed by birds, and the soil's microscopic life can break down the mulch, converting it to food for your plant's roots.

As long as this mulch is not turned into the soil, a balanced release of nutrients will be sustained. If the mulch is turned, a temporary loss of nitrogen may slow this process and stress your plants. If the mulch layer needs some aeration, it is better to punch it with a manure fork and lift slightly. This will introduce more oxygen without disturbing the layers. A mulched garden is best weeded by hand. This may sound like a horrible job to those used to clean cultivated ground, but in a mulch the plant roots are usually near the surface, where there is adequate food and water. A simple pull and most weeds will come out, roots and all. If weeded on a regular basis, a mulched garden is easy to maintain.

To create more activity in a mulched garden, alternate layers of finished compost, perhaps adding some extra bloodmeal or fishmeal, with layers of mulch, such as shredded bark, rotted sawdust, leaves or evergreen needles. This will help keep your nutrient levels, including nitrogen, higher, and decomposition will be intensified.

Mulched gardens usually suffer less drought stress because there is so little evaporation of water from the surface, but problems can develop. Be sure when starting a mulch program that the soil is sufficiently damp. Once the mulch is in place, it takes a tremendous amount of water to penetrate a thick layer of mulch. If the mulch material is dry, wet it. If you are suffering a severe drought, check regularly under the mulch to be sure water is still available. A rainfall may not reach the soil layer where it is needed once the mulch has dried down to the soil level. A mulched garden suffers less from low soil temperatures in winter and high soil temperatures in summer, but a mulched soil will stay fairly cool during the growing season, and frost will also take longer to leave the ground. These can be advantages or disadvantages. Where high soil temperatures or early thawing are desired, a mulch can be detrimental. As always in gardening, knowing your needs will help dictate the methods you employ.

PLANTING

The roots of a tree or shrub grow downward to obtain water and anchorage, but the largest percentage of roots grow outward, usually within 20 in. (50 cm) of the soil surface. It is here that food is most available and oxygen levels are highest. With this in mind, be sure that the hole you dig for a new tree or shrub is deep enough to accept the root system, but more importantly, that it is wide enough to permit lateral growth. This is particularly true in heavier clay soils, which may prevent the easy penetration of roots into the walls of the dug hole.

Abrupt changes in the texture or density of a soil can create problems. If your tree or shrub is planted in a relatively loose textured soil but is underlain with a dense clay or rock layer, its roots will not easily penetrate the lower soil. Such a shallow root system may be a problem with larger trees, particularly in windy areas. If possible, try to break through or at least loosen the dense lower soil.

Perhaps a more common situation occurs when transplanting potted plants. Most container mixes are quite light and porous, often with a high percentage of peat moss or bark. If such a light mixture is surrounded by a dense soil, root penetration can be very poor and the plant will not have access to the nutrients and water contained in the surrounding soil. Particularly prone to such problems are fine-rooted plants such as rhododendrons, azaleas and blueberries, but any plant can suffer under these circumstances. A light potting mix will also dry out readily if not kept

When planting a tree, the hole should be deep enough to accommodate the root system. Providing as wide a hole as possible will aid root growth near the surface, where most feeder roots are located. A mulch will help insulate the soil, prevent soil compaction and provide a source of organic matter. Stakes driven into unmoved soil should be used to support larger trees.

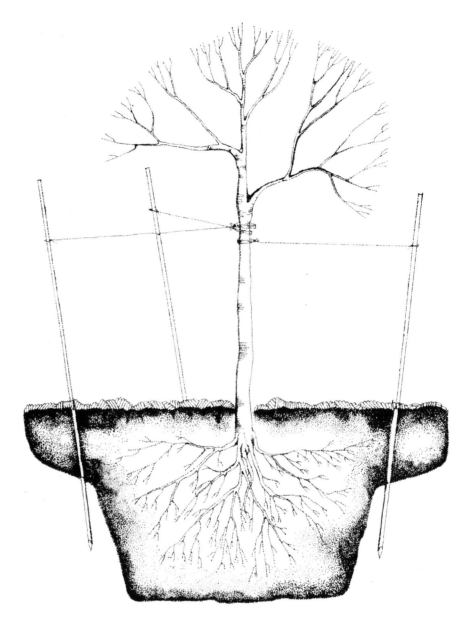

well watered. Once they are dry, light mixes, such as peat moss, are difficult to re-wet. Even though you may water the plant, the water will tend to run around the dry rootball without penetrating to the interior. Be sure such rootballs are thoroughly soaked before planting, and keep up your watering regularly. When planting bare-rooted plants in a clay soil, you can create a similar situation by filling the hole with light materials such as peat moss or compost. Many planting guides insist that you should always incorporate such materials into any planting hole. It has been demonstrated that in a situation such as this, it is better to use the existing soil around the new plant roots and put the composts and such on the surface as a mulch. Light-textured soil amendments in heavy soils often create more problems than they solve. If the soil you are planting into is light, incorporating soil amendments should not present problems. A plant, potted or balled in a clay soil, will grow into lighter soils, but it is still best to use a soil that is somewhat denser near the edge of the rootball to avoid an abrupt change in soil texture.

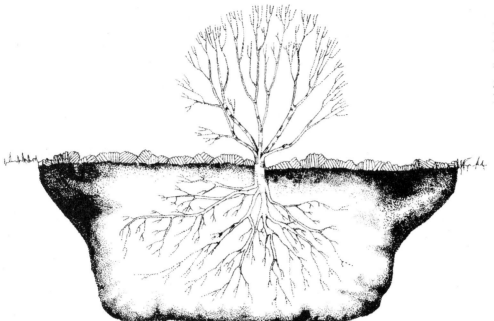

The width of a planting hole for any shrub is at least as important as depth since most shrub roots grow close to the surface. Mulches are beneficial.

When you buy a potted plant, it may have been growing in its container for some time. When you remove the plant from its container, check to see if the outside roots are coiled around the perimeter of the rootball. If they are, gently comb or tease out the roots so they can be spread in the planting hole. If the roots are so tight or fine as to be impossible to pull out, it is better to take a knife and make several shallow vertical cuts to the rootball than to leave it. In this way, new roots will form and will grow outward into the surrounding soil. Plants that were rootbound and never dealt with properly will often never grow roots beyond their original container shape. This causes many transplanting failures.

When filling around your newly planted tree or shrub, be sure to pack and tamp the soil around the roots so that no air pockets remain. These spaces can cause roots to dry and do not allow the roots to establish good contact with the soil for water absorption. They also affect the stability of the plant, particularly if it is tall. It is useful to slightly dish the top of the planting hole so that your early waterings are pooled directly above the plant roots and do not run off sideways. When your planting is complete, be sure to thoroughly saturate the soil once. This will help to settle the soil and should remove any remaining larger air spaces, creating good contact between the roots and soil particles. Continue to water often enough that the soil stays damp, but not soggy, because good aeration is also important. Adequate water is the most essential requirement for successful transplanting. If you plant in spring, be sure to water well throughout the entire growing season. The next year's growth will repay your attentions.

Fertilizing should be directed at root growth the first season. A critical element in creating a strong root system is phosphorus, and an excellent source of phosphorus is bonemeal. Adding a handful or two of bonemeal to the soil surrounding your new plant's roots can be very useful to the transplant. Compost, either worked into the planting soil or on the surface of heavy soils, will give the new plant a good supply of nutrients immediately and in the future. Be careful not to use high-nitrogen granular fertilizers in close proximity to a transplant's roots. High levels of nitrogen can burn the tissues, especially when the plant is not absorbing enough water. If you prefer granular fertilizers, use them on the surface and delay their use until the plant is established in its new site, usually a month or so after planting.

Trees of any size should be staked. If the tree is small, a single stake might suffice; however, larger trees should be staked with three stakes. Metal stakes or 2 in. by 2 in. (5 cm by 5 cm) wooden stakes are usually used. Drive these stakes into undisturbed soil so that they will stand firm in the wind. It is usually advisable to use a soft steel wire for anchoring the trunk to the stakes. Use a suitable length of rubber hose to protect the trunk from the wire. Tighten the three wires until they are snug and no more. After a year, remove the wires. If you feel they are still needed, loosen them to accommodate growth. A tree that is staked will not rock in the wind; rocking impedes good contact between the roots and soil and will affect growth. If you fail to stake, particularly in a windy site, you may find yourself looking at an uprooted tree in the near future.

PRUNING

Pruning should be guided by a sense of purpose. Wading into a tree or shrub knowing only that you "should" prune can be harmful to the plant and often to the visual pleasures of your garden. It is also true that lack of pruning can often keep a plant from reaching its potential or, in some cases, can threaten its health or survival. There is nothing inherently good or bad about pruning.

It is presumptuous of us to assume that we can improve on a plant's innate ability to grow itself, but the techniques of pruning can be used to alter the shape or density of a tree or shrub to suit our desires. It can be a tool to stimulate them to grow in certain ways or produce more flowers. Pruning can be used to stop the spread of disease or to create conditions that help to prevent disease infection.

Know what you are trying to accomplish by pruning a tree or shrub. Once you have established this purpose in your mind, your cuts should be guided by a basic understanding of how trees and shrubs function. When you prune, you disrupt the flow of materials within the plant, and this disruption can work either toward the accomplishment of your goals or against it.

Trees and shrubs, like animals, have a circulation system. However, rather than veins and arteries, they have layers of specialized cells. These cells pass materials from cell to adjoining cell through their walls. The absorption of water and nutrients begins in the outermost cells of the roots. Here delicate strands of tissue called root hairs absorb through their walls water and other substances the plant needs. This liquid moves toward the center of the root, where it is filtered through a specialized layer of cells. It then moves upward into the stems. The loss of water in the leaves, called transpiration, combined with the pressure of the atmosphere on the water in the soil enables the plant to create a pressurized column of water. In some plants, such as the Douglas fir or giant sequoias, this column can exceed 300 ft. (90 m) in height – a truly astounding bit of hydraulic engineering!

In trees and shrubs, the layer that moves this sap upward is called the xylem. If you were to peel away the bark, then peel away the green inner bark, you would reach the woody portion of the stem or trunk. This is the xylem, providing both support and a transportation system upward from the roots. When you tap a maple tree to obtain sap for making maple syrup, you are tapping into the xylem layer. Constant pressure from below fills the drill hole and eventually your bucket.

As the tree or shrub ages, the older xylem cells die. The dead cells become empty pipes, connected end to end, through which the water moves. Only those xylem cells on the outer edge are alive. Here the cells reproduce, forming new layers covering the old cells, gradually increasing the girth of the stems and roots. Because the process is rapid in spring and summer, then slows as fall approaches and stops during winter, the pattern that is created is ring-like. Examining the rings in the trunk of a felled tree shows the yearly growth and how rapidly that growth took place.

As this column of xylem pipes grows upward, groups of these pipes break off in various directions, stimulated by the presence of light and the genetic blueprint of each species. These become branches. From the branches, more pipes branch off to form smaller stems and still other pipes branch off to form leaves. The pipes separate in the leaves and fan out in patterns unique to each species, growing a webbing of cells between the pipes. The water and minerals that have been pushed upward filter into these webs. Specialized cells on the leaf surface, called stomata, form; they open and close, allowing water to leave and gases to be absorbed and expelled.

The cells of the leaves contain specialized bodies called chloroplasts, which contain chlorophyll. This unique substance is arranged into crystalline patterns that trap red and blue light and reflect green light. The green color of plants is caused by light bouncing off these chlorophyll solar collectors. Water from the roots and carbon dioxide taken in through the stomata are transformed within these collectors into sugar, in which the energy collected from the sunlight is trapped. Oxygen, a waste product of this reaction, is released back into the atmosphere through the stomata.

The sugars are fed into another layer of pipes, called the phloem or cambium. When you peel back a section of bark, the phloem can be seen as a thin green layer. This layer is a series of long cells connected at their ends by plates with tiny holes that allow the sap to pass from cell to cell. These cells, when full of sugar, are slightly pressurized. Where growth is occurring in the plant, the sugar is used, and as it is, the pressure in those cells drops. The pressurized phloem layer pushes more sugar-rich sap into these cells, and in this way the sugars are distributed throughout the plant. Because the roots do not produce food but are large consumers of food, there is a general movement down the inner bark of the plant toward the roots. Eventually the food reaches the outer layers of the roots and the fine root hairs, which are growing outward and downward, absorbing water and nutrients as they delve. The circle is completed.

When you prune a tree or shrub, you are severing bundles of pipes that carry water to the leaves and food throughout the plant. The reaction of the plant to this disruption of its natural growth pattern will depend on the type of plant, the condition of the plant, the time of year and a host of other influences.

Bear in mind that pruning is a dwarfing process. Removing stems removes some of the plant's ability to produce food. You also eliminate the stored food contained within the stem. Even though a pruning cut may stimulate vigorous growth near the cut, the plant will not produce as much total growth as it would if left unpruned. It is important, therefore, to assess the vigor and health of a tree or shrub before you prune so that you can gauge how well the plant can recover from the pruning. A plant that is already stressed may suffer irreparable harm from a severe pruning. With its capacity to produce food diminished, it may not have the capability to feed both the stem portion of the plant and the roots. Remember that the roots are the last part of a tree or shrub to be fed. A plant that has been pruned beyond its ability to recover may not be able to feed its roots and the results of a weakened root system may not show up until the following year, when growth will be poor. If the root system has been starved, the plant will die.

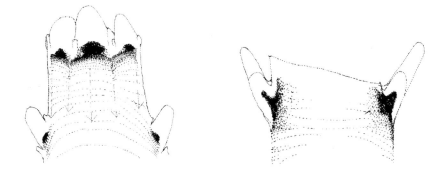

The terminal buds produce growth auxins that elongate the cells above their production sites. These auxins migrate downward. As they travel, they stimulate the production of ethylene in the side (lateral) buds. The ethylene inhibits growth in these buds. When the terminal is removed by pruning or by natural events, the auxin concentrations drop and the ethylene is no longer produced, stimulating the production of auxins, and therefore growth, in the side buds. Once these buds begin producing auxins and growing, the newly formed side buds below them are inhibited from growing.

There are other forces at work when you cut into a tree or shrub. Trees and shrubs, like all living things, produce chemicals that regulate their growth. Your pruning cuts can change the amount or the distribution of these substances. If all the buds on a plant grew at the same rate, the plant would soon become a congested mass of material. Chemicals that control growth in trees and shrubs are called auxins. Auxins are produced in various parts of the plant, including the terminals of the stems. The cell walls above the sites of auxin production in the growing tips of plants become more plastic, allowing them to elongate and grow upward. These auxins are released in minute amounts but can be toxic if their levels are allowed to build up. Instead, they move down the stem during growth. As they move downward, they stimulate the production of a chemical called ethylene in the side, or lateral, buds. This chemical prevents the lateral buds from starting into growth. The same auxins that stimulate growth above their production sites repress growth below them, a bewildering yet very efficient use of materials. Normally, therefore, most growth takes place in the terminals of the shoots. When you cut the terminal off a stem, a cut called "heading back," you remove the production sites of these auxins and the concentration of auxins drops. Without these auxins, the ethylene is no longer created, and the lateral buds are stimulated to grow.

You can see this response when you head back a branch in spring. Soon vigorous new shoots have formed on the buds below the cut. Once in growth, each of the new shoot tips will begin producing auxins to inhibit the newly forming lower buds from growing. The overall result is a much bushier plant, with more stems than would have been produced if the heading cut had not been made. This usually results in the production of more sites for flower buds to develop as well. The intensity of this response will diminish as the season progresses. This is why such pruning cuts will stimulate vigorous long shoots in spring, but less vigorous shorter shoots in summer and fall.

Although pruning is a stressing process, plants have an astounding ability to cope with this stress, and with proper attention to soil quality, water, space and light, your plants should not unduly suffer and may sometimes benefit from pruning. Always be guided by the thought that you should prune only as much as is necessary to accomplish your purpose.

Pruning Shrubs

As a gardener you probably have an appreciation for the diversity of the shrub world. Generalizations about pruning shrubs are, therefore, difficult, but some general principles can guide you.

Many spring-flowering shrubs form their flower buds during the previous year. An example of such a shrub is the forsythia. As soon as temperatures rise in spring, the flower buds expand and you are treated to a golden yellow display that heralds a new season. Other examples are the lilac and rhododendron. It is best to delay pruning such shrubs until just after flowering. In this way, the shrub will be able to form flower buds on the new growth for the next year's show. Pruning them in the early spring, fall or winter will deprive you of the floral show that is the reason for growing them.

Shrubs that form their flowers on the new season's growth are generally best pruned in the fall, winter or early spring. An example of such a shrub is the potentilla. If a potentilla is pruned just prior to growth in the spring, the vigorous new shoots will still form flowers on the new growth. Other examples of this type of shrub are repeat-flowering roses and spireas. Bear in mind, however, that when you remove branches, you often reduce the number of flowers that will be produced.

There are many reasons you might want to prune your shrubs. As shrubs grow older they can become very dense. When light is reduced in the center of the shrub, growth there becomes limited. Growth and flowering occur only on the outer shell of such shrubs. By removing older stems in a thinning process, you allow light into the center of the plant and stimulate growth and, ultimately, flowering. Thinning can also be used to reduce the height of a plant. If the older, taller canes are removed, the younger, lower shoots will remain. Height is reduced without a sheared look. This technique is useful for informal shrubs such as mock orange, bridal-wreath spirea or lilac. Thinning can also encourage better air movement within a shrub, often reducing the incidence of fungal disease. Shrub roses are an example of plants that can benefit by such treatment. When thinning, it is best to remove the entire cane as close to the ground as possible, or to remove stems cleanly where they branch off a larger stem. Such cuts will not leave stubs, are not readily noticeable and will maintain your shrub with its natural form intact.

If you want to create geometric forms with shrubs or if you are creating clipped hedges, you will need a different pruning technique. In such cases you are shearing or heading back all stems that are growing beyond a predetermined flat or curved plane. When you head back stems, the response will be determined by the type of plant, the time of year and the amount removed. If such cuts are made when the plant is dormant, the new growth will be vigorous in the buds just below the cut. When the cuts are made in summer, the response is more often the production of short lateral or spur growth, usually related to the production of flower buds. This initiation of flowering wood is most likely a survival response. In order to protect the species, a "threatened" plant tries to produce seed. Maintaining a clipped shrub or hedge of shrubs may involve both spring and summer pruning, but generally summer pruning will not stimulate "wild" long shoots, as will spring pruning. This makes summer pruning preferable in situations where you are trying to maintain shrubs at a certain size.

If you are shearing shrubs, remember to keep the bottom of the shrub wider than the top. If you try to maintain a vertical wall or ball shape, the bottom of the shrub will not get sufficient light and the shrub may lose its bottom leaves entirely, becoming open and ragged at the base. You may want to do some annual thinning on sheared shrubs as well. Continual shearing will create a dense outer shell with little growth on the inside. By doing a small amount of thinning each year you can stimulate more new interior and lateral growth, creating a somewhat thicker layer of growth. Where shearing has been carried out for many years this outer shell can be very thin. Damage to the shell can result in a hole that can be hard to fill again. In

Deciduous Trees

Amur Maple, *Acer Ginnala* (p. 36)

Sugar Maple, *Acer saccharum* (p. 37)

Striped Maple, *Acer pensylvanicum* (p. 37)

Red Maple, *Acer rubrum* (p. 37)

Serviceberry, *Amelanchier species*
(p. 38)

Toba Hawthorn, *Crataegus mordenensis* 'Toba' (p. 38)

White Ash, *Fraxinus americana* (p. 39)

Green Ash, *Fraxinus pennsylvanica* (p. 40)

Butternut, *Juglans cinerea* (p. 40)

When pruning a hedge, be sure that the base is always wider than the top. A straight sided or undercut base will not have sufficient light for proper growth and will end up leafless and open.

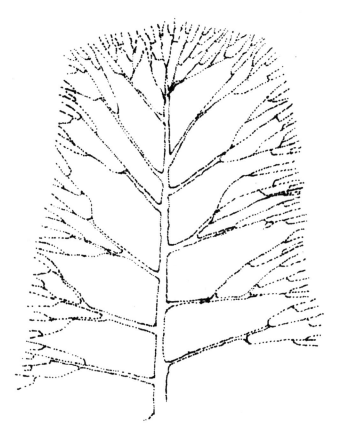

such cases you can pull one or more healthy stems into the hole with twine. Use a twine that will rot; synthetic twines may strangle the stems later. Stimulated by light, these stems will soon fill in the hole.

You may want to create greater density and flowering in a shrub. Certain practices allow you to do this without necessarily creating a clipped or formal look. Plants that can benefit from such techniques include rhododendrons and azaleas. These plants, if left unpruned, can often grow into lanky specimens with somewhat sparse flowering. They form their flower buds on the terminals of the stems during the late summer as growth ceases. After they flower, you will notice several vegetative shoots growing from just beneath the spent flower. If you pinch the very tips of these shoots in early summer, after they have grown some but before they set their terminals, you will stimulate the formation of short lateral growth below the pinched tip. The result will be a fuller plant. You may lose some flowering the next season because many of these shoots will be vegetative, but by the following year there will be many more shoots and a sizable increase in the number of flower buds. If you pinch back the plants when they are young, you will be able to create a more compact bush that, when in flower, will become a cushion of color. Pinching terminals is a technique that can be used on many shrubs to produce these same results. It does not reduce the shrub's food production very much and is not overly taxing to the plant.

Another pruning technique does not involve cutting wood, but removing spent flowers. A plant's raison d'être is to produce seed. Even though seeds are generally small in relation to the size of the plant, they consume many of the nutrients produced by the plant in their creation. When you remove a spent flower, you divert energy that would have gone into seed production into the formation of new shoots,

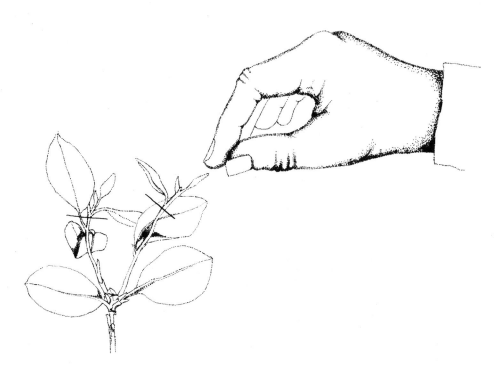

The new spring growth of a rhododendron can be pinched to create more lateral shoots, which will create a denser plant and eventually more sites for flower buds.

and in the case of repeat blooming shrubs, such as many of the shrub roses, into the production of yet more flowers. Nearly any shrub can benefit from this technique. Obviously if the fruit is an important part of the ornamental quality of the plant, you will not want to remove the flowers. But when the fruit is not of importance to you, removal of spent flowers can create better vigor and increased flower production in the future.

Pruning techniques allow you to manipulate the form and often the performance of a plant, but bear in mind that the most important decision you make is what plant you put in which space. A vigorous shrub will always be difficult to maintain at a small size. A small plant may never fill the space it is given. Trying to train an upright shrub to grow outward, or vice versa, will lead to frustration and the destruction of the shrub's natural form. Choose plants that will fit the location and try to work with a plant's natural growth patterns. With an understanding of a plant's habits, you can prune to enhance its form.

Pruning Deciduous Trees

You are in a grove of large trees, silent except for the sound of wind through the branches and chattering squirrels. The long straight trunks of the trees have long ago lost the branches that existed when the young sapling grew up toward the light. The crowns of the trees on the ceiling of the forest receive nearly all the sunlight, leaving only dim reflections for the understory plants that can survive the diffuse light. In the nearby field a large tree grows alone. Its thick stems start from near the ground and round to the top, a dense, squat mass of branches. These are the same species of tree, but where light is available, the branches remain vibrant and covered in leaves. In the forest the lower branches, shaded by the forest canopy and their own upper branches, slowly die. The forest tree is a long tall specimen, the field tree wide and spreading. Our reactions to the two shapes are different. Pruning allows us to manipulate trees to create different reactions, different "feelings."

By removing the lower limbs of a deciduous tree, you can access the space under it. You can sit under such a tree, feeling protected by its canopy. You can plant shrubs or perennials underneath the tree and create a more complex space, with other textures and colors. A long trunk can give the tree an impression of height. A tree with its lower limbs left will appear more solid, more attached to the ground. It can be approached but not entered. It is important when growing a tree to decide what kind of "feeling" you want to create. Your decision will govern whether to prune and if so, to what extent.

Although you can shear trees into geometric forms, you will more often be thinning out branches. This involves cutting to the main trunk or to another branch. The way this cut is made is important to the proper healing of the wound. If you examine the point at which a branch grows out of a trunk or another branch, you will notice a raised ring of tissue at the juncture. When you cut a branch, make your cuts as flush as possible, but leave this ring. The ring is rich in auxins, which stimulate callous tissue to grow and cover the wound. When pruning heavy branches, be sure to make an initial undercut some way out from the final cut. Then cut above the undercut. This first cut will prevent the limb from tearing the bark downward as it falls. Afterward make a final cut just beyond the bark ring.

Although there are many products on the market to cover pruning cuts, it is now generally accepted that most of these products do not speed recovery. More often they inhibit healing, and if the wound dressing separates from the wood, a perfect environment for fungal infection can be created. Proper pruning cuts made with sharp tools and the antiseptic rays of the sun are usually sufficient.

Many species of deciduous trees are prone to weak crotches. Typically a branch will be growing quickly and at a narrow angle. Bark becomes trapped between the trunk and branch, and as the branch grows and becomes heavier it becomes more

When pruning a large limb, use an initial undercut (1) to prevent tearing of the bark when cut 2 is made. The final cut (3) should be made close to the trunk but should preserve the slightly swollen collar at the limb's base.

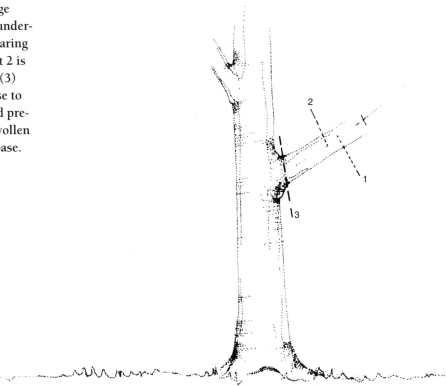

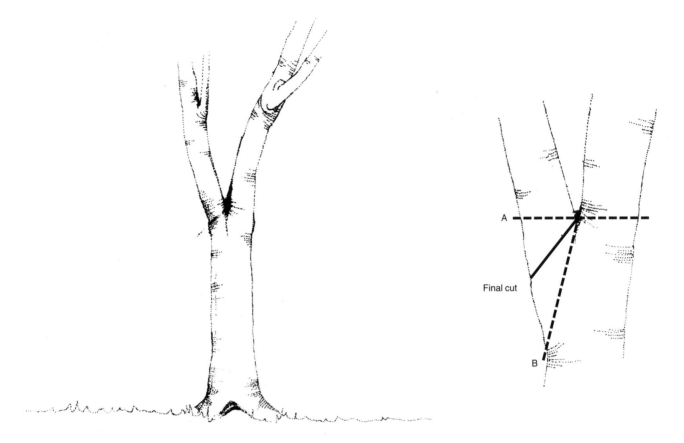

likely to split away from the trunk, with grave consequences for the tree's future. If these branches are removed when young, you can prevent such occurrences and the tree will not suffer from stress. Removing older branches with narrow crotches will be more stressful to the tree, but such action is often justified when this type of crotch threatens the long-term health of the tree, for not only can the branch split the tree under loads of ice or snow or in wind, but as the crotch grows, water becomes trapped between the branch and trunk. The bark rots and fungus can enter the heart of the tree.

In spring pruning, you will often encounter sap bleeding from the wounds. Certain species of trees such as maples and nut trees will bleed profusely, often for weeks. Although opinions vary as to the extent this stresses the tree, I prefer to err on the side of caution and prune trees that bleed heavily late enough to avoid the heavy spring sap flow, but early enough that the wound has time to heal its edges before the cold shuts growth down. Fall and winter are acceptable times for trimming most trees, but in cold climates there is more risk, particularly in more tender trees. Tissue that has not sufficiently healed can be injured by frost, giving a place for cankers and other fungal infections to gain entry.

If disease does gain a foothold in your tree, be sure to act quickly. Old pruning stubs or breakage points can become infected with organisms such as cankers. These infections can work their way into healthy tissue and damage your tree. Diseases such as Dutch elm disease, *Juglans* dieback in butternuts or fireblight in apples can be eliminated from your tree if caught early. Be attentive to your trees and be aware of dead

When pruning one of the limbs of a V-shaped crotch, your final cut should be made at an angle approximately mid-way between the line perpendicular to the edge of the limb (A) and the line parallel to the edge of the remaining limb (B). Initial cuts should be made as shown in previous illustration.

or sickly looking foliage that signals the presence of disease. Delay in dealing with the problem may mean the difference between life and death for a treasured tree.

Pruning techniques allow you to create garden sculptures. Trees can be molded into living works of art, blends of the tree's habit and your pruning talents and personality. With imagination and a sharp blade, a shapeless mass of branches can be converted into a delicate silhouette. You may be able to approach a tree and know instantly how you want it shaped. When you are not sure, it is best to be patient. You cannot undo a poorly planned pruning cut. Study the tree. Contemplate its growth patterns. Come back later. The time will come when you will know what you want.

Manipulating the amount of fruit that a tree produces can also be a technique to alter the growth pattern. An apple or flowering crab on a dwarf root is an example. The dwarf root will stimulate the tree to produce fruit early in life. If these early fruit crops are allowed to develop, the energy spent on seed production will result in less vegetative growth and the tree will be smaller. If you remove fruit just after it forms on young trees, the energy will be diverted to shoot growth and the tree will gain more height. When it reaches the desired height, you can allow it to fruit heavily and the tree will slow its growth.

Pruning Evergreens

Often in pruning, less is more. Pruning is often unnecessary and can even delay the desired results. My advice to those planting an evergreen is to care for the soil, remove competition and let it go. Except for the removal of broken or dead branches, pruning is usually not needed.

There is a trait among humans (some might call it a flaw) that lets us believe we can improve on nature's systems. Imagine you are visiting a nursery to purchase a young spruce. The young, vigorous tree has widely spaced whorls of branches and looks a bit open and sparse, not the perfect dense cone you had envisioned – but remember that this small, open spruce may eventually grow 20 ft. (6 m) wide and could someday dwarf a two-story house. Left on its own, this tree will quickly grow both wide and tall. By trying to create a dense tree at this stage, pruning will actually delay the time it takes it to attain its large stature. Shearing the young spruce will create a system of closely spaced and dense branches that may actually be a handicap as the tree grows older. The widely spaced whorls are appropriate for the eventual spacing of the long horizontal branches that will develop. The tree's growth pattern has been developed over the ages to ensure a healthy, long life. Interfering with this pattern is often detrimental to the tree.

You may want to produce a dense, conical evergreen. Before you plant, however, consider how the variety you plant corresponds with what you want to create. If you are looking for a small, dense evergreen, find one that is naturally dwarf and dense. Your job will be much easier with such a variety than with a larger variety that is continually wanting to break free of the confinement imposed by the pruning shears.

Shearing evergreens is best done in early summer when the new growth is expanding but the terminal buds have not yet set. In pines this new growth is referred to as candles. The pine shoot grows upward, setting a new terminal bud surrounded by several lateral buds just underneath. If you prune after the terminal buds have set and growth has ceased, new buds will not form and the result will be stubs that eventually die. Instead, prune the candles as they grow, and you will reduce the amount of annual growth. Because the candle is still actively growing, it will produce

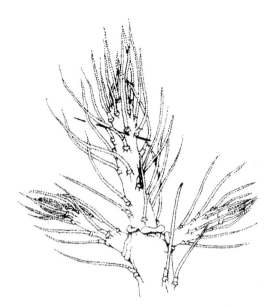

a new whorl of buds on the cut tip. Growth will commence from this new terminal the next year. After several seasons the tree will become quite dense. Evergreens such as Mugo pine are often sheared to create cushiony mounds in the landscape.

Evergreens such as spruce, juniper and cedar are different in that their shoots have a terminal bud and many lateral buds along the side of the shoot. These evergreens can be pruned when dormant or when growing. The general practice is similar to pines, and most growers prune these evergreens during active growth. This promotes rapid healing of the cuts and good bud formation. Many of these evergreens when sheared will form dense hedges for windbreaks, privacy or decoration. Those so inclined can fill their lawns with geometric shapes as plain or as fanciful as their imaginations allow.

Thinning branches can be very useful in the creation of sculpted evergreens. The inspired removal of certain portions of such specimens can give a special character to your garden. While some may turn a Mugo pine into a dense, uniform mound, others might create a layered composition of branches and needles resembling green clouds scudding across an imaginary sky. It is this diversity of styles and approaches to plants that makes gardens such exciting and unique environments.

Left: The shoots (candles) are cut during active growth in early summer. Right: Buds will form on the edges of the cut surface, which will grow the following summer.

Root Pruning

A less common but nonetheless effective means of pruning involves cutting portions of the root system. This has the effect of reducing the uptake of water and nutrients, thereby dwarfing the top. These techniques are used in bonsai. The tops of bonsai plants are pruned quite heavily each year. By root pruning as well, you can further reduce the amount of growth in the plant and prevent the stimulation of vigorous vegetative growth. If this is done carefully in stages, and if the soil is kept fertile, bonsai plants can be successfully maintained at a small size indefinitely.

Root pruning is a technique used extensively in the commercial production of plants. Nurserymen often prune the roots of plants in the field to produce a profusion of smaller feeder roots where the roots are cut. This makes for a smaller rootball that is easier to transplant when it is dug. When a plant is dug and transplanted into a container, its roots are often pruned. This creates more lateral roots, resulting

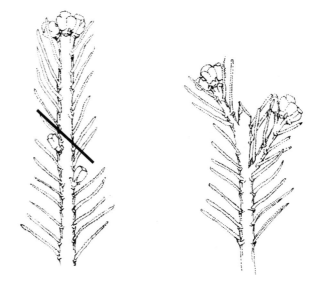

A fir or spruce forms side buds. Pruning can be done either during active growth or when dormant.

in a more confined root mass that is easier to transplant into its final home. As always, these pruning techniques can be detrimental to the plant if carried to extremes. Extensive root pruning or poor digging techniques that eliminate much of the root system will result in poor growth or even death.

In the home garden a sharp spade plunged in a circle around the drip line of a young tree or shrub can reduce top growth and will help confine the root system to a smaller area, thereby reducing competition with nearby plants. This technique is also useful when you plan to transplant a more established tree or shrub. If root pruned during the summer, it will grow smaller, finer roots before freeze-up and you will be able to dig it with a more compact rootball either that fall or in the following spring. Such confined rootballs will transplant easily because the plant will have already adjusted to the loss of the cut roots while still in the ground, and any stress during transplanting will be minimized. When root pruning, it is wise to disinfect your tools regularly to prevent spreading root-borne diseases such as crown gall from plant to plant.

It is an interesting fact that a plant can generally recover from a severe root pruning more easily than from a severe top pruning. This aside, roots are the part of the plant that absorb most of its water and minerals. Root pruning will tax a tree or shrub in the same way top pruning does. Prune only what you need to accomplish your goal.

The Tools

When pruning trees and shrubs, it is important to suit the tool to the task. If you are pinching back new shoots, a thumb and forefinger may be just the thing. A sharp knife can also be used to perform lighter tasks. Most pruning work can be accomplished with a good pair of pruning shears, called secateurs by many. Larger limbs may require long-handled loppers or pruning saws. To perform the toughest jobs, you may have to heft an ax or chainsaw. With a bit of common sense and a few simple tools, you should be able to handle nearly any pruning job.

If you are a serious gardener, take heed of advice that applies to any tool purchase: buy the best. Pruning tools are not major investments, but good tools usually do cost more than cheap tools. You'll notice we said "cheap." An inexpensive tool, if well-

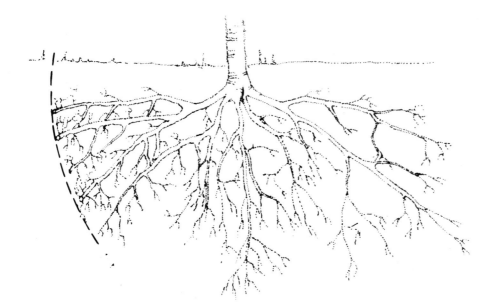

When roots are pruned during transplanting, or while the plant is in the ground, several smaller roots will form at the cut ends. In this way you can keep the root system in bounds. This will also restrict top growth. Root pruning is often used to create a smaller fibrous rootball that is more easily transplanted the following season.

made, is a bargain. A cheaply made tool does not perform its job with precision and ease. A cheap tool is never a bargain, no matter the price. A good craftsman keeps his tools in good condition. A pruning tool that is dull or rusty is not only frustrating to use, but can tear the fibers of your plant, inviting in disease and other problems.

DISEASES AND INSECTS

There is no end of recipes available to "cure" your trees and shrubs of the diseases and insects of the world, but these recipes do not address the problem of why the disease or insect attacked in the first place. By understanding the processes going on within and around your plants, you will know how to change conditions to reduce the incidence of these problems. Disease and insect damage can occur because of a weakness in a plant species or an individual within the species that allows the entry of a disease or insect. Damage can also occur when a plant is stressed by environmental conditions or the intrusion of the gardener. Knowing why something is happening increases your chances of solving the problem.

Like animals, plants have defenses to deal with stresses. Their leaf pores open and close as the availability of water changes. This protects the leaf from drying. The growing layers of trees and shrubs produce corky cells that fend off the drying wind and piercing insects, and protect the roots from abrasion as they push their way through soil particles. When attacked by insects, plants can produce substances that will deter further feeding and others that help heal the wounds. These are all defenses against conditions that threaten their integrity and health.

Diseases and insects need energy for growth and reproduction. They find it in other living things. Sometimes the victims are your trees and shrubs. If conditions are suitable when a fungus spore lands on a leaf surface, the spore opens. Its unique genetic pattern produces a sharp, probing group of cells that pierce the tough outer cells of the leaf surface. Soon it is growing in the cells of the leaf's interior, protected from the outside world by the very layer of cells it pierced to gain entry. Inside the leaf the filaments of the fungus fan out, feeding on the sugars contained in the plant's cells. Before the leaf dies, the fungus forms another pattern of cells and pierces the leaf's outer layer again. This time specialized cells disperse new spores into the air, new spores that may land on new leaves. The species is continued. Similarly the bark borer uses its special genetic patterns, such as chewing mouth parts, to bore through the outer bark of trees so that it can feed on the sugars of the inner bark. In doing so it feeds itself but interrupts the flow of food within the tree. If the damage is extensive, the tree can die.

The ability of a species and individuals within the species to fend off the probing of diseases and insects will in great measure determine how successful your plants are in your garden. Choosing plants that rarely succumb to such attacks will avoid many problems. Information about a plant's susceptibility to disease and insects is a valuable tool for a gardener.

Individual plants that have the genetic ability to fend off attacks can still fall prey to diseases or insects if they are stressed and their normal defenses are weakened. Winter is perhaps the most common stress. Each winter your trees and shrubs must prepare their roots and shoots to endure subfreezing temperatures and fluctuations between freezing and thawing temperatures. In order to survive the severe low temperatures of the north, hardy plants have developed the ability to move excess water out of the cells and into the spaces between the cells. The film of water that remains around the important parts of the cell is so thin that it can remain elastic even in extremely low temperatures. This phenomenon is known as supercooling. The more adept a plant is at supercooling, the farther north it can be grown.

If a plant is unable to prevent the formation of ice crystals in its cells, the cell walls will rupture. As soon as temperatures rise, the cell will begin drying. Fungi and insects will also have access into the cell and will begin feeding and breaking down the dead tissue. These organisms can then gain entry into living tissue. Roots can be similarly injured. Deprived of water and nutrients from the roots, the tops, even if unharmed by winter, come under great stress. Without the active transport of water, food and growth regulators, the cells become weakened and more subject to attack. In some cases specialized chemicals used to repulse insects will not be transported where they are needed. Insects and disease can gain a foothold and the eventual result may be the death of the tree or shrub. The snow and ice of winter can also tear down branches and rub off bark. In spring insects enter the wound and begin eating the sugary cells. Spores of fungi, bacteria and molds carried in the air currents may land on the new wound and grow into the plant. Although it may be difficult to prevent mechanical damage from ice and snow, you can choose plants that are hardy in your climate. More tender plants, even if they survive the winter, can be routinely damaged by low temperatures and the result will be an increase in disease and insect problems.

The gardener can create many stresses. You cultivate, prune, disperse substances and move plants within the garden. Each of these activities can adversely affect plants in your garden. Cultivation can increase the soil temperatures in summer, killing roots. Pruning can cause the introduction of diseases into live wood. Fertilizers and pesticides can change the type and numbers of species living in the soil. Transplanting can mean a loss of water and minerals to a plant. All these things have consequences. Sometimes the consequences lead to stress that allows disease and insects to enter the plants.

You can help your trees and shrubs keep the plant eaters at bay by creating the best conditions possible for your plants. A vibrant living soil will provide not only the essential minerals but also the trace elements that help build an active internal defense system. Clean air and water will keep the systems of food production and distribution working properly. Sunlight will provide the energy needed for photosynthesis. It may also help to destroy fungus and molds. Good air circulation can protect plants from frost damage, which can open wounds to infection, and it can prevent the germination of plant diseases by keeping plants drier. Pruning infected stems on a tree or shrub can stop disease from spreading. Mulches can keep the soil from drying and create an environment that fosters the growth of soil life. Just as you regulate the food your children eat and the conditions in which they live to protect them from diseases and insects, so your work in the garden should be geared to providing the necessary conditions for healthy plant growth. The key is prevention.

Your purpose should not be to eliminate insects and funguses in a garden. Indeed, the healthiest environment for your trees and shrubs is one in which the number of such species is immense, for it is the diversity of life that creates a balance, where no one species is dominant. Most insects and diseases in your garden are benign or helpful to your plants. Spiders patrol the branches, seeking out the sucking aphids or the winged flies that chew the growing tips. Tiny mites travel the convoluted ridges of tree barks attacking other mites that suck the juices from your trees. Thousands of species compete for food in the soil. As they die, their bodies are attacked by other insects, and in the process, your plants are fed. Specialized fungi called mycorrhizae in the soil interact with tree and shrub roots to provide food and water. They often deter attacks on plant roots by soil insects and can be antagonistic to fungi that feed on plant roots.

You cannot prevent pests from entering your garden, but when they arrive, the predators of those pests arrive as well. They may begin eating the pests immediately or they may lay their eggs among the pests to hatch at a later date. If you set out to kill the pests and your solution kills their predators as well, you are working against your own interests. You should endeavor to find solutions that target your pest as specifically as possible. This may be as simple as destroying caterpillars by hand, or as sophisticated as using chemical attractants called pheremones to lure the pests into traps.

When you spray a garden with a powerful toxin to kill a particular insect, you kill most of the insects, some of the soil life, and sometimes even bird life. You have totally altered the complex makeup and distribution of life within the garden. You may eliminate an insect pest for a brief time, but in doing so, you have eliminated many of the natural enemies of the pest. If it re-establishes itself, it will not have the normal controls that keep its populations in check, and the result can be an even more intense buildup of the pest.

Your garden is an immensely complex ecosystem. Each part of the system depends on other parts of the system to function. By destroying parts of this system, you set off a series of events whose consequences are not possible to predict. Each time we interfere to "correct" a problem, we create more problems that need solving. Encouraging diversity in the garden is the most logical way to prevent an individual disease or insect from becoming a problem. Spend energy ensuring your plants' needs for sunlight, water, space and nutrients are being met. Most importantly, relax. If your plants are well cared for, the natural systems of control will prevail. Respect the ability of the natural world. Take action where action is needed but recognize that there is also a place for inaction.

Even if you have done everything you can to reduce the stresses that promote disease and insect problems, there may be times when you feel you must take some type of action. If you are plagued with a particular insect or disease, there are "recipes" that can help you become a predator without unduly disrupting the garden environment. Because of the number of species represented in this book, it is impossible to detail every disease and insect. The following groups of diseases and insects represent the type of damage that can occur in trees and shrubs.

Diseases and Recipes to Control Them

Mildew

Mildews usually appear in the later summer, particularly if humidity has been consistently high. Position susceptible plants in open areas where they receive good air circulation and, if necessary, prune to open the plant to better circulation.

Mildews germinate on the leaf surface and penetrate into the leaf tissue to feed on the sugars. When the fruiting bodies grow, the leaf appears to be covered with a white or gray powder or fine down. To prevent the germination of mildews on leaves and fruits, you can spray them with a solution of 1 tbsp. (15 mL) of wettable sulfur powder to 1 gal. (3.8 L) of water. Add two drops of a pure soap to help the sulfur mixture stick to the leaves. The sulfur creates an acidic film on the leaf surface, preventing the germination of the mildew spores. A solution of 1 tbsp. (15 mL) baking soda (bicarbonate of soda) to 1 gal. (3.8 L) of water and two drops of a pure soap creates an alkaline surface on the leaf and destroys much of the existing mildew, as well as preventing further germination.

Canker

Cankers are fungi that take advantage of an injury to gain entry to the live tissue of plants. Cankers are usually noticed when their fruiting bodies, most often orange bumps, appear on the injury. Pruning cuts, winter-damaged wood, torn branches and similar wounds can give the cankers a place to germinate their spores. Although they initially feed on the dead tissues, many species of canker move into living tissue and can cause a great deal of damage if not stopped. Dead or injured

Left: Cankers enter through an injury in the bark and feed on the living tissues. Initially the bark will appear sunken and discolored. Soon the wound becomes an open lesion. Right: Cankers often gain entrance from a pruning cut or broken limb, soon spreading into healthy tissue. The presence of small round pustules is a telltale sign of its presence.

tissues on trees and shrubs should be neatly removed with sharp pruning shears or a knife. It is wise to sterilize your shears between cuts with rubbing alcohol or bleach. Observation and quick action are the keys to stopping cankers before they become problems.

Cankers that occur on a main limb or trunk should be scraped down to the inner wood and the edges of the canker injury trimmed back to healthy green tissue. The entire surface should then be covered with a layer of water-based paint such as a latex or acrylic. If any canker remains, it will be smothered. Keep an eye on the site to be sure there is no re-growth and that the edges of the wound start to grow back toward each other. Making a delicate slice along the edges of a larger wound each spring, removing only the outer bark to expose a thin line of green cambium, will increase the amount of callous produced, closing the wound more quickly. Even large wounds can be closed in this manner although it may take several years.

Rust

Rusts are fungi that attack the leaves and inner barks of shrubs and some trees and can be a particular problem with some rose varieties. It overwinters on dead leaves and shows up as an orange powder on the undersides of leaves and on stems. Remove and destroy any rust that appears, using pruning shears that you sterilize between cuts, and bury or burn fallen leaves from susceptible plants in the fall. Another option is to cover fallen leaves with a good layer of compost and/or mulch to prevent the spores from getting to the air. To prevent further infection, after pruning out infected tissue, spray with the sulfur or baking soda mixtures described in the mildew section.

Bacterial Infections

Bacterial infections can be devastating to plants. They often move into a plant and cause irreversible damage before being noticed. Symptoms include wilted foliage and liquid-filled pustules on the bark. A classic example is fireblight, which affects apples, pears, mountain ash and other related trees. The bacterium usually enters the growing tips of the trees and moves downward through the phloem tissues. The pustules ooze, releasing spores that are carried to other plants by insects or birds. Be watchful for any wilting leaves on the terminals of growth as this is usually the first sign of a bacterial infection. Prune the affected branch some distance below the observable infection and burn the prunings. Sterilize your pruning shears between cuts. Watch the branch for any further sign of damage and remove it if necessary.

Virus

Many different types of viruses are present in our trees and shrubs. Just like viruses in humans, viruses can be living within plants without causing any damage or even showing detectable symptoms. However, they can become virulent when a plant is stressed. Some viruses affect the plant immediately, causing symptoms such as oddly shaped leaves, unusually colored foliage or misshapen stems. It is virtually impossible for the average gardener to rid a plant of a virus. If you find a plant exhibiting symptoms such as described, and it seems clear the symptoms are not caused by soil conditions or other factors, it is best to destroy the plant in order to protect other plants from being infected by sucking insects who can transfer the virus from one plant to another.

Insects and Recipes to Control Them

Aphids

These soft-bodied small insects attach themselves to tender new leaves and the growing tips of plants. With their sharp tubular mouthpiece, they pierce the phloem tubes and suck the sugary sap. They can appear in great numbers and may distort or kill young growth if they are not stopped.

Aphids are often associated with ants, who use the aphid excretions, called honeydew, for food. The ants protect the colonies from predators in order to protect their food supply – an example of animal husbandry not that different from our own.

Aphids multiply exceedingly rapidly to ensure species survival because so many predators live to eat them. The list of predators includes spiders, ladybugs, syrphid flies and a host of other insects. Birds too feed on aphids.

Usually, patience pays off when dealing with aphids. Insects such as ladybugs and syrphid flies lay their eggs in the developing colony. Just as you think you can no longer bear to let them be, the aphids will start turning to dried husks, victims of the larval stage of these ruthless predators. In approximately five minutes, a ladybug larva can grab its hapless victim, pierce it and suck the living juices from it. Within a short time, the colony is destroyed and the larvae move to the next colony.

If you cannot wait for nature to take its course, sprays such as insecticidal soap will destroy most of the aphids. They will, however, destroy their predators as well, and if used on a continual basis, the aphids that can survive the soap will reproduce to produce generations of soap-resistant aphids. If you can reach the affected portions of a tree or shrub, a good strong spray of water is a simpler alternative. Once washed off the leaf, most of the aphids will not make it back to the plant before being consumed by other insects, but newly arriving aphids will find a site where the predators have been rousted as well. Soon their numbers will multiply again. This is a case where inaction is often the best alternative.

Scale

Scale insects are sucking insects that secrete a protective waxy coat around themselves, making it difficult for predators to reach their soft parts. Scale can occur in great numbers and can completely cover the surface of stems. They often attack trees that are under stress and, once established, create even greater stress as they suck the needed sap from the plant. Scale insects are seen on many species of trees and shrubs. Trees such as elm, willow, apple and pear can be attacked. Shrubs such as cotoneaster, dogwood and lilac are favorites of scale.

The larvae of many predators emerge from eggs laid in the colonies of their hosts. Here a ladybug larvae forages among the aphids it will devour at the rate of one every five minutes.

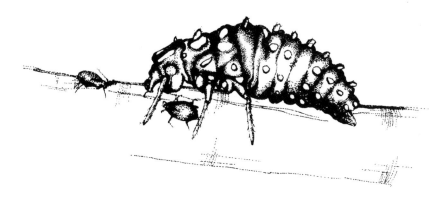

If an infestation is heavy enough to cause damage, a dormant oil can be sprayed on the stems in spring just before the buds open. Scale also is susceptible to sprays of insecticidal soap when they move in the spring. The females lay their eggs under the protective scales and in the spring these young emerge to seek their own position on the stem. These young "crawlers" will be emerging when bridal-wreath spirea is in full bloom and the lilacs have just finished blooming.

Leaf Miners

Leaf miner eggs are laid by tiny wasp-like insects inside the leaf. The hatched larvae tunnel through the leaf's interior to feed, leaving brown trails. Trees such as birch, alder and hawthorn are often attacked by leaf miners. Because the larvae feed within the leaf, they are virtually immune to sprays. Some commercial growers use systemic insecticides to combat leaf miners; however, these materials are among the most toxic of insecticides and may have a damaging effect on the tree if used improperly. Generally leaf miners do not kill their hosts. Because these are one of the more difficult pests to treat with biological methods, it is perhaps wisest to leave nature to keep populations under control and let nature "have her due."

Caterpillars

There are innumerable species of caterpillars that feed on the foliage of trees and shrubs. Species that feed singly are usually of little consequence. The problem species usually feed in large numbers. These include such examples as the gypsy moth, eastern tent caterpillar, forest tent caterpillar and the web worms. These insects have cycles. Their populations build for several years until the infestation is quite heavy, then fall dramatically as predator populations increase. There is little you can do to influence these larger population fluctuations, but you can act to limit damage in your own garden. Learn to identify the egg mass stages of the caterpillars. Fall is a good time to search for them. They are most often found attached to small branches or on the trunks of trees. Destroying them at this stage will save a tremendous amount of work later. The tent caterpillars should be destroyed as soon as the tents appear. When they are small, a simple wiping up with a pair of gloves will suffice. They feed outside the tent in the daytime and return to the tent for protection at night, so the best time to destroy the nests is just before dark or just after sunrise. Do not use fire or solvents to destroy the nests. This will often harm your tree far more than the caterpillars would.

Beetles

Some beetles attack foliage on trees and shrubs. A prime example is the Japanese beetle. This beetle can be hand-picked, but keeping up with a large population is difficult. A natural control, milky spore disease, can be spread on the soil to destroy the overwintering larvae. This has significantly cut down on this beetle's numbers. Luckily for northern gardeners, very cold winters usually limit the population of this insect.

Beetles that attack young foliage and flowers include the blister beetle. These long beetles sometimes feed on the blossoms of trees such as the plum and can severely affect a fruit crop. Hand-picking is advised. A simple aid is to spread a sheet on the ground under the tree and give the trunk a quick shake. Many of the beetles will fall onto your sheet where they can be easily gathered up. It is interesting to note that during another phase of its life the blister beetle feeds on grasshopper eggs – an example of an insect that on the one hand is a pest, while on the other hand works to control another pest.

Beetles that bore under the bark of trees usually appear after some other damage has occurred or when trees have been stressed. An interesting example is the elm bark beetle. This beetle builds its egg chambers in the cambium tissues of weak or sickly trees. Although not especially destructive to healthy trees, they do feed on the twigs of healthy trees in the vicinity of sickly trees. In doing so, they act as a carrier of the Dutch elm disease, which is fatal to the elm. This is an example of an insect that was of little consequence until a disease, introduced by man's activities, hitched a ride with the beetle.

Most beetles feed on other insects or soil life and will not cause any great harm to your trees. Be observant and hand-pick those that feed on your plants.

Borers

Borers drill through the bark layer of trees and shrubs to feed on the inner bark. Borers attack trees such as locusts, poplars, apples, birches, ashes and elms. The entry holes can usually be spotted a short distance up the trunk. A telltale sign is a small pile of sawdust at the entrance or on the ground under the hole. If caught early, a fine wire fed down the hole will usually puncture the larva and kill it. A dilute bleach solution can also be poured down the hole. If not caught, the borers can completely ring the cambium layer with their feeding and egg-laying activities. The result is usually severe dieback or the death of the tree.

The borers chew their way into the stems of their hosts and eat the living tissues, often with fatal results for the plant.

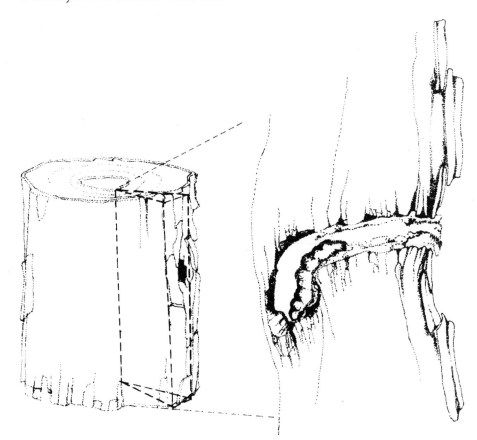

2

Deciduous Trees

THE LEAVES OF DECIDUOUS TREES BLOW AWAY ON THE AUTUMN BREEZE, but they offer delights that the evergreens cannot. You can choose a tree with limbs that are straight and true or that writhe like climbing snakes, with barks that range from rugged scales to skin as smooth as silk. Their leaves are long or short, they're round or flat, or thick or thin. Leaves of lime or deepest shades of green can turn, in fall, to hues of yellow, orange or red. These trees have flowers, some so tiny only passing ants or searching eyes will see, others so profuse or large they cause us pause whenever they're in view. From the deserts to the far reaches of the north, deciduous trees decorate our gardens with a multitude of forms and textures as varied as the gardens in which they grow.

AMUR MAPLE

Acer Ginnala

The Amur maple has its origins in Manchuria where the immense Siberian forests meet the Pacific Ocean. Winters along the Amur River can be cold and cruel, and the Amur maple is well adapted to such conditions. It is a small tree, one suited to landscapes requiring a tree with presence but without the overwhelming size that most shade trees attain.

    This tree is generally multi-stemmed and creative pruning can produce silhouettes of great character. If you train it from youth, and allow only a single stem, it will form a delicate small tree reminiscent of the lovely Japanese maples, but far hardier. Its leaves are three-lobed and smaller than its other maple relatives. When the shortened days of fall arrive, the leaves transform to ruby-colored wafers that gleam as if metallic. Amur maple's fall display is a curtain call that entices you to return for the next year's performance.

Royal Star Magnolia, *Magnolia stellata* 'Royal Star' (p. 41)

Red Jade Flowering Crabapple, *Malus* 'Red Jade' (p. 42)

Rudolph Flowering Crabapple, *Malus* 'Rudolph' (p. 42)

Selkirk Flowering Crabapple, *Malus* 'Selkirk' (p. 43)

Tower Poplar, *Populus canescens* 'Tower' (p. 43)

Red Oak, *Quercus rubra* (p. 44)

Bur Oak, *Quercus macrocarpa* (p. 44)

American Mountain Ash, *Sorbus americana* (p. 45)

Littleleaf Linden, *Tilia cordata* (p. 45)

Staghorn Sumac, *Rhus typhina*
(p. 46)

Cutleaf Sumac, *Rhus typhina*
'Laciniata' (p. 46)

Japanese Tree Lilac, *Syringa
reticula* (p. 47)

Conifers

Calgary Carpet Juniper, *Juniperus sabina* 'Calgary Carpet' (p. 49)

Japanese Garden Juniper, *Juniperus procumbens* 'Nana' (p. 50)

Yukon Belle Juniper, *Juniperus horizontalis* 'Yukon Belle' (p. 50)

Waukegan Juniper, *Juniperus horizontalis* 'Douglasii' (p. 50)

Arcadia Juniper, *Juniperus Sabina* 'Arcadia' (p. 51)

Blue Danube Juniper, *Juniperus Sabina* 'Blue Danube' (p. 51)

Swedish Juniper, *Juniperus communis* 'Suecica' (p. 51)

Tamarack, *Larix laricina* (p. 52)

Little Gem Spruce, *Picea Abies* 'Little Gem' (p. 54)

Nest Spruce, *Picea Abies* 'Nidiformis' (p. 53)

Weeping Norway Spruce, *Picea Abies* 'Farnsburg' (p. 55)

Ohlendorff Spruce, *Picea Abies* 'Ohlendorffii' (p. 54)

Dwarf Serbian Spruce, *Picea Omorika* 'Nana' (p. 56)

White Spruce, *Picea glauca* (p. 55)

Iseli Fastigiata Blue Spruce, *Picea pungens* 'Iseli Fastigiata' (p. 58)

Colorado Spruce, *Picea pungens* (p. 57)

SUGAR MAPLE

Acer saccharum

When you watch the boiling, clear, sweet sap of the maple tree turn into sticky sugar, you are watching the distilling of a food made from the water, air and sun's warm rays. This could be done with sap from many trees, but it is the sugar maple's sap we crave. As the equinox arrives in spring, the maple pushes water laden with stored sugars from the roots upward, bathing the vital skin and buds with sweet sap and commencing growth that terminates in leaves. Like the piercing aphid, we drill our holes into the tree and take a share of its sweet sap.

The sugar maple is a rugged tree that is at home on rocky slopes or well-drained ground. Its deeply furrowed flaking bark and ascending branches are well known from the mountains of Tennessee to the Acadian forests of Ontario, Quebec and the Maritimes. The symbol of the maple leaf appears on everything from packaged meats to Canadian flags. Perhaps no other tree is so synonymous with the north.

The sugar maple is famous for its syrup, its form, its hardiness and, most of all, its fall colors. So spectacular are the brilliant yellow, orange and red leaves that millions of people ride into the hills of eastern North America to witness the spectacle of a hundred thousand colored trees emblazoned on the rocky slopes. This is the annual pilgrimage of the leaf peepers, witnesses to a sight that heals their souls as well as any holy shrine.

STRIPED MAPLE

Acer pensylvanicum

The shade garden is a challenging site to design. Although your choices are more limited, the proper plants can make a shade garden as visually stimulating as a sunny garden. There are many herbaceous perennials and shrubs available for shady situations, but very few deciduous trees can be used as understory elements in shady sites. A tree that is being discovered by designers and nurserymen for these situations is the striped maple.

This relatively small tree has a somewhat irregular form with ascending branches that arch gracefully with age. If grown in full sun, the trunk is usually short and branches low, but grown in the shade its trunk is long and slender and the branches high. The three-lobed leaves are large and showy, but the most intriguing aspect of striped maple is its bark. As a seedling its bark is red, but quickly turns to green with thin white stripes that stand out, even from afar.

The striped maple grows best in cool, moist, well-drained soils. It will grow in either sun or shade and, though tolerant of acid soils, will benefit from lime where the soil is very acid. This tree is relatively hard to find but is worth the search. It is one of our least appreciated hardy, native trees.

RED MAPLE

Acer rubrum

Picture, if you can, a river island, flooded in the spring. The water sits for weeks or even months, draining only after winter's snow has joined the open sea. On the island grow scores of trees with fat red buds that open early, a nectar feast for wild bees. The smooth new bark is red as well. These are red maples – trees that crave the damp, the swampy ground. If you've a site that's wet and needs a tree, here's a likely candidate.

Red maple grows quite large, so must be given lots of room. Although double stems occur, it generally grows quite straight, with a single trunk that branches low or high, depending on the light. The young red bark turns silver-gray as it matures, forming flaky scales in older age. Although a denizen of damper sites, red maple can be grown on well-drained ground as well, provided it holds some moisture.

Although the fresh new wood and winter buds are red, the tree is best known for the red of its three- to five-lobed leaves in fall. While the sugar maple shifts from green to shades of yellow and orange, the red maple's leaves always turn to red, a last hurrah before the fall.

SERVICEBERRY

Amelanchier species

In the spring many of the hedgerow's stark and twisted winter forms are hidden by cloaks of bloom. Among the first to burst its swollen buds is the serviceberry, called by some the juneberry, by others the Indian pear, by others the mayflower, by still others the saskatoon, and I'm sure by others, other names. Whatever name you choose, this harbinger of spring is a delight. Its showy flowers are the main reason gardeners plant this sinuous small tree, but there are other considerations that demand the attention of the discriminating grower.

The smooth gray surfaces of the twisting branches form a graceful winter silhouette. In spring the new leaves have a blush of red that soon transmutes into a deep and healthy green and in fall turn shades of red and yellow. The fruit is a delicious summer treat and in many colder regions has become a commercial crop. The small blue-black rounded fruits are as sweet as the blueberry and can be made into pies and jams of outstanding quality, but you have to be on your guard to beat the birds to this late summer harvest. On top of this, the serviceberry is at home in either sun or dappled shade.

The small scale of this tree, the many ornamental qualities mentioned above, and its outstanding hardiness and health make it one of the most useful plants available to the northern gardener. Find this oft-neglected native and let it add a multitude of delights to your garden space.

TOBA HAWTHORN

Crataegus mordenensis 'Toba'

Some trees appear to dance, with stems that writhe and dip and follow paths more winding than the straighter, simpler trees. To me they're special in a garden, giving pause to those who pass and have the time to contemplate such things. The wild hawthorn rarely grows a single trunk and often forms small clumps, closer to a shrub than a tree. Whether or not you choose to influence its growth by pruning, this smallish tree adds flowers, fruits and form to the garden.

Hawthorns are the denizens of open land and often form the hedges separating farmers' fields. Give them light and well-drained ground and lime where the soil is acid. Like the apple to which it is related, the hawthorn will repay the extra care of compost and some lime with the riches of white flowers and red fruit.

Hawthorns grow as native plants in parts of North America, Europe and Asia. You can find hawthorns for your garden on a local hill or you can choose one of the numerous selections that have been grown in gardens for centuries. The northern grower must be wary, though. Hawthorns such as 'Paul's Scarlet' can be found in nurseries and catalogs galore, but in the northern reaches it often lives a short and tortured life. Better to search for tougher ones like the 'Toba'. Gardeners often voice sharp objections to the thorns that can grow on the hawthorns, and those not wary of these dangerous spines may have to live with scars attesting to their lack of care. No need to worry with this rugged, hardy hawthorn. 'Toba's' slightly kinky branches grow just leaves and flower clusters, which when open transform the stems to garlands of white double flowers more akin to small carnations than to apple blooms.

The flowers of the 'Toba' undergo a subtle change as the petals age. The new blossoms, fresh and white, slowly flush with pink, until the tree is a parasol of flowers to rival the more famous, but tender, flowering cherry. This treat is available to nearly any northern gardener, for the 'Toba' is at home in the coldest sites. Because this tree is nearly always grafted, try to find what root it's grafted on and be sure it's hardy. Even though the 'Toba' buds do well in cold, a tender root can spell disaster in a cold and snowless winter.

The 'Toba' has a sister plant named 'Snowbird'. This variety is similar in form and flower and is even hardier, but keeps its snow-white color till the petals fall.

WHITE ASH

Fraxinus americana

As September's days draw near October, the ashes upon the hills turn deep purple. Their glossy leaves succumb slowly to the wind and strong thick branches emerge as their colored coverings scatter to the ground. White ashes can grow trunks that several people, hand to hand, cannot embrace. In the forest, they tower overhead, with long, straight branchless trunks that disappear into the canopy above, where neighboring trees compete for light. The slightly corky bark forms shallow interwoven ridges that are as firm and unyielding as the legendary wood that grows beneath the light gray bark. The resilient wood has long been prized for everything from handles and bentwood chairs to baseball bats.

If you need a tree with presence and stature, white ash is a good selection. White ash are often found near water, whether that be a stream, a pond or shallow water table. Although a body of water is not necessary for success, be sure your soil will provide the ash with moisture all year. It is not fond of dry soils, but prefers the moist leafmolds of a woodland site. It will grow as well in heavier soils that hold water well. This makes it a valuable tree for clay soils. The white ash forms a wide shallow root system in such soils and can prosper. Add lime to acid soils and, as is the case with nearly every tree, improve soil fertility for optimum growth. Be sure the ash is never planted where late spring frosts occur. Its early growth is sensitive to frost, so choose a site where cold air will drain away on still spring nights.

Some claim that ash leaves rubbed on a mosquito bite will afford relief. For many gardeners, this may be reason enough to plant this hardy tree, but there are many other reasons. Watch how the compound leaves split the light and leave a dappled shade. The strong gray trunk bends and tolerates the wildest winds. The autumn colors decorate the garden by their depth. With space and time, this ash can grace your land with a strength and solidity few trees can match.

GREEN ASH

Fraxinus pennsylvanica

The branches of this ash have a thrusting, rigid look. The stiff branches of the green ash grow more upward than outward, creating a slender egg-shaped frame, one useful where width is limited or the design calls for a narrow tree. Cities where winters are frigid often use green ash as a street tree because of its form and ability to withstand both cold and difficult urban conditions. Indeed, this tree is both tough and adaptable.

In its native habitat the green ash often grows alongside rivers and lakes, sometimes to the water's edge. Although it will form a fine tree in well-drained soils, green ash makes its best growth on dampish ground and will even tolerate heavy, wet clay soils that would kill the roots of most shade trees.

Green ashes often set a heavy crop of long, thin-bladed seeds that hang on into winter like clusters of miniature canoe paddles rustling in the slightest breeze. Soon the wind and snows of early winter rip them from their wiry stems. On the ground they may become meals for foraging mice and squirrels or, for the lucky few, new green ashes. If you do not care for seeds, there are a number of selections that are sterile and set no seed. Among the best known are 'Cimarron', 'Marshall's Seedless', 'Patmore' and 'Summit'. All are hardy and have tidy forms.

BUTTERNUT

Juglans cinerea

Many of us are drawn to nut trees, feeling part squirrel as we collect the fallen nuggets from the ground, knowing that inside each convoluted shell lies a kernel of flavor both rich and rare. The more familiar nuts such as hickories, chestnuts and walnuts often fail where winters are intense and growing seasons short, but one nut tree grows in places far too cold for these famous trees. It is the butternut. The butternut is closely related to the better known black walnut and Persian walnut. Its large leaves are compound, the many leaflets giving it a tropical appearance. In good soils it grows rapidly, eventually becoming a large and spreading tree. The bark, when young, turns from brown to silver-gray. On older trunks, flattened ridges weave an intersecting pattern.

This tree is not for every garden or every gardener. Butternuts are large and need a deep and fertile soil. Their welcome nuts are another chore for those who do not want them on the lawn. As well, the roots release a substance that injures certain plants. It is best to grow it in a large and open space and avoid underplanting with perennials or shrubs. The butternut has been devastated in the wild by a fungal disease called *Juglans* dieback. While untended trees can eventually be felled by this disease, it is not a problem in the cultivated garden. The disease starts at the tips of branches and slowly works its way downward. All that is needed to stop the disease is to prune below the infected portion. The disease works very slowly and is easily eliminated by a sharp pair of shears or a saw in the hands of an observant gardener.

The nuts themselves are covered in a sticky husk of green that quickly turns to mushy black. The husks are used for dye, so protect your hands with a pair of gloves if you plan to peel them. To open the dark, grooved shells, stand the nuts, point up, on a hard surface such as a stone or a cement floor. Give the point a sharp rap with a hammer and the halves will split apart. Usually the meat will have to be picked out, but some trees release their meats whole. The flavor of the nut is second to none. The name butternut says it all. If cracking nuts is not your thing, the squirrels will love you all the more. Despite some drawbacks, if you have the space and a yen for nuts, few trees are as rewarding as the butternut.

ROYAL STAR MAGNOLIA

Magnolia stellata 'Royal Star'

Outside the wind is howling, sending what little snow there is swirling around the brown and gray stems of the 'Royal Star' magnolia. Its fuzzy, drab green flower buds are tightly sealed against the cold. The temperature hovers at -22°F (-30°C). Surely this is no place for a magnolia. Yet as the warmth of May does its magic, and the sap swells the buds to bursting, we are witness to the sight of pure white petals unfolding into a most rare flower, an immense arrangement of rounded straps that release an aroma into the air that is unlike any tree in the garden, a fragrance for memories that will last far longer than the dancing molecules of scent in the wind. The flowers punctuate the many stems that thrust upward from the ground. It is a thrilling sight for a northern gardener.

The magnolias of the south are playthings in the north, tender trees whose fate is death when left outdoors. But a very few are worthy of a try for those who love to test the limits of their site. Among the best is 'Royal Star', but another worth a try is a hybrid of the star magnolia named 'Merrill' (*Magnolia* × *Loebneri* 'Merrill'). These are among the toughest of the tough, but tough as they are, they are still tender in the far north. Treat them with extra care. Face the trees east if possible, away from north and west winds. Give them soil that is rich and loamy, but avoid nitrogen-rich fertilizers, which will produce soft, watery growth. Keep the soil moist, but never wet. Prune them very lightly. Although they grow as trees, they are somewhat shrub-like and often have many lower limbs. Give them every advantage you can. It is important, as well, to be sure the plant you obtain is on its own roots. If it's grafted, the chances of the rootstock being as hardy as the top are very slim. Sing to them if you think it will help. If they do survive, the pleasures they give are worth every shovel of compost. Although it is perhaps wisest to stick with only hardy plants, few gardeners can resist the temptation of forbidden fruits. 'Royal Star' is a plant that may be worth the gamble.

FLOWERING CRABAPPLE

Malus species

The gnarled branches of an ancient apple tree silhouetted against the sky is a sight to stir the most jaded garden designer. Few trees have such potential as landscape material, yet the apple is often overlooked as an ornamental. On larger sites, apples are usually given a place of their own in an orchard, but they are equally deserving of a place in your garden.

As the frosts of early spring disappear, the fragrant blossoms of the apple, both white and pink, fill the air with their perfume. This display alone would endear the apple to the gardening world, but the fruit that follows lasts much longer and is just as ornamental. Although this volume cannot devote space to the many apples you can grow, suffice it to say that any hardy apple can be a delight to the eye as well as the palate, but the group known as the flowering crabs has a special place in the northern garden and it is this group of apples that we will treat as ornamental.

The apple grows on sites where sunshine is plentiful and water is available but never sits. It is not particularly demanding, but as with any garden plant, richer ground will grow a better plant. Do not neglect to lime acidic soils.

There are hundreds of hardy crabs from which to choose, but if you seek the very healthiest, your selection dwindles considerably. Fungal diseases such as apple scab and mildew attack many varieties. Bacterial diseases such as fireblight can kill trees outright as well. With crabs, your choice of variety can be critical to success.

Varieties

RED JADE
Malus 'Red Jade'

The winter outline of 'Red Jade' is reminiscent of a cascading fountain, with its slender branches looking like frozen rivulets of water bouncing over an invisible jumble of rocks. In the warmth of later May, the prolific blossoms nearly hide the coppery stems in a sea of white, but it is the many small deep red, rounded fruits that give this crab its name. The kinky nature of 'Red Jade' is an aberration that sets it apart from other crabs. Its striking form provides you with a living, growing sculpture for your garden. You can also change the impact of this, or any, weeping tree by using different training methods. Most weeping trees are staked in the nursery so that they will have a high trunk. Growth beyond that point will fall toward the ground, but without staking, a variety like 'Red Jade' will form a ground cover, gradually mounding up with time. Cascading over a wall's edge, 'Red Jade' can create a powerful image. If trained with a low stem, the tree becomes the vernal equivalent of a spring issuing out of the ground. Thoughtful pruning can produce truly unique specimens. By branching out from the norm, you can create personal and exciting designs.

RUDOLPH
Malus 'Rudolph'

The use of Latin names for plants flusters many people who find the long names difficult to master. Like most seemingly difficult things, however, constant usage dissolves the mystery. This universal botanical language crosses all political boundaries and allows botanists everywhere in the world to know they are talking about the same plant. Among these many names, there is one that is a real mouthful for those not familiar with sounds of the Slavic languages. It is a very important name too, for this is the species that has given many of the finest flowering crabs their color. The species is *Malus Niedzwetzkyana*, the red-veined crab. The red and pink flowered hardy crabs called the Rosyblooms have resulted from hybridization with this tongue-twisting species. One of the hardiest, healthiest and showiest of these crabs is 'Rudolph'. This vigorous upright crab was developed by Frank Leith Skinner of Dropmore, Manitoba, a prolific breeder of super-hardy plants. He selected 'Rudolph' out of a group of hybrid seed and named it after the storybook reindeer because of its dark red buds, which open into vibrant pink blossoms. The fruits grow to resemble pie cherries, and if you grow 'Rudolph', you will no doubt be asked what kind of "cherry" it is.

SELKIRK
Malus 'Selkirk'

Everyone makes a tremendous fuss over flowering crabs in bloom. This is entirely justifiable, as there are few trees that can compete with a crab in full flower. As with all wonderful moments in life, however, this glorious profusion of color lasts but a short time. What is often overlooked is that many flowering crabs are as showy in fruit, and this spectacle lasts far longer than the flowers. 'Selkirk's' fruits are blood red, with a sheen that sets them apart from the average crab. You first notice the fruit in summer, and as they mature, they grow more showy. When fall winds sweep away the leaves, 'Selkirk' has its Christmas decorations hung and, like a child unwilling to stop celebrating, leaves them hanging far into the new year.

It would be unfair to forget 'Selkirk's' flowers, however. Just as the swallows return from their southern sojourn, the tree bursts into a glorious show of intense pink. For a week or more, the arching branches are virtually hidden in a cloak of petals. Underneath this pink blanket unfurling buds reveal new reddish leaves that turn bronze-green as they expand. 'Selkirk' has a color for all seasons.

In winter I often ski across the fields with my young son. On days when the sun is warm enough to unfreeze apples that still cling tenaciously to certain trees, we stop at the hedgerows and suck the sticky sweet fermented juice from these sagging brown bags. We delight in comparing each tree's flavor and finding those we like the most. We are, perhaps, alone in our appreciation of an apple most would never notice, let alone eat. But they are the poorer for it.

TOWER POPLAR

Populus canescens 'Tower'

Poplars are not popular. Their short life span and weak wood, combined with the sticky flowers that some species drop on cars and walkways, seem to have consigned them to the farmstead hedgerow or the abandoned lot. One of the few poplars to have survived horticultural shunning is the famous tall and narrow 'Lombardy' poplar. This plant has always had a place in gardens everywhere. It is a plant that is universally recognized and rightly so. This Italian native is surprisingly tough, but in the coldest sites its rapid early growth is soon replaced by dying wood. In just 10 years or so the tree is nothing short of derelict. Before you write off the poplars as a group, you need to hear about a new kid on the block. This 'Lombardy' cross has all the fine points of its more tender parent and the toughness of the native poplar that provided it with hardy genes. It is the 'Tower' poplar.

As it reaches upward, the branches of this tall, lean tree twist slightly, like corkscrews that have been pulled straight up, leaving just a hint of their former look. The architectural quality of this plant is obvious, making it an excellent choice for linear arrangements or where geometric formality is desired. Walking among a group of 'Tower' poplar, planted to imitate a natural stand, can provide a unique experience, somewhat like walking in a forest of leafy skyscrapers.

Be careful not to cultivate poplars too deeply. If the roots are cut, suckers will develop from the point of injury. This plant will do well in most soils but grows best where moisture is not far from the roots. A word of caution: poplars have extremely long roots and can invade and even plug septic fields or wells. Keep them well away from the outdoor plumbing. Pruning is usually not necessary with the 'Tower' and preserving the base branches will add to the impact of this columnar plant. With the exception of removing dead wood or perhaps giving it a light thinning as it ages, this tree takes care of itself quite nicely. Poplars will tolerate some acidity; however, growth will improve if lime is added in very acidic soils. As with most poplars, the growth is astoundingly rapid. Plant, step back and watch this amazing selection head for outer space.

BUR OAK / MOSSYCUP OAK

Quercus macrocarpa

The bur oak is found in many parts of eastern North America, most often growing in river valleys, where the soils are rich and deep, but occasionally on upland sites. It is the most northerly growing of the white oak group and forms a large tree with deeply furrowed bark and a rugged branching structure that gently kinks and twists, bringing Chinese landscapes brushed on paper scrolls to mind. Most hardy oaks have leaves with lobes that end in points, but the leaves of the bur oak have rounded lobes that vary in length and width with each tree. The branches often have a corky bark, giving younger trees a fascinating texture. Its acorns are encased in fringed cups that nearly envelop the nuts inside. Squirrels appreciate the acorn's sweet white meat, for rarely can you beat them to the ripened crop. This hardy tree is not only healthy in the wild but also grows where air pollution might kill others, making it a good choice for urban sites where its large height would not cause problems.

With all these attributes you'd think the bur oak would be for sale at every garden center. Alas, this tree is hard to find, and you will need to chase one down, but something desired and hard won is always sweeter to obtain.

RED OAK

Quercus rubra

From little acorns mighty oak trees grow. If you've wandered through a grove of old red oaks, you know how true this old saw is. The oak is one of the northern forest's premier trees. On well-drained sandy ground or hills with rock or gravel soils, the red oak's thick black trunk grows straight and tall. In open fields the branches can be low and often grow nearly as thick as trunks. The glossy leaves are dark and thick, sometimes hanging on into winter, rustling in the breeze like camel-colored cards.

This is a tree for larger yards. It grows both wide and tall and casts a shade that none but understory plants will tolerate. The leaves of the oak are rich in tannins and create an acidic mulch. This forms a perfect site for azaleas and rhododendrons, which prefer a filtered light and need an acidic soil.

The rain of acorns in the fall is welcome food for squirrels and a toy with endless possibilities in a child's hand. The fashioning of boats and caps and fairy pipes has always been a rite of youth for those who live where oak trees grow. A child at play in a forest or a garden is a child rarely bored, one whose thoughts of youth are thoughts of Earth.

AMERICAN MOUNTAIN ASH

Sorbus americana

Robins sometimes fall to the ground completely drunk after eating too many of the fermented deep red berries that hang in crowded clusters in the mountain ash. Perhaps it is a fitting final bash before the tiring journey to the south. Although a favorite food of many birds, it is always sad to see the berries go, not only because it portends the cold to come, but when in fruit there are few trees that compare in splendor to this rugged, hardy tree. The flowers of the mountain ash are as showy as its fruit. In early summer after the leaves have matured, the ivory flower clusters hang on the branches' ends, much like icing on a cake.

This smallish tree most often has a spreading vase-like form with several stems, but can easily be grown with a single trunk. It is ideally suited to smaller yards and is tolerant of many soils. The European mountain ash is much more common in the nursery trade and makes a beautiful but larger tree. Its berries are more orange in color as a rule, with an upright oval form. The European species suffers more from cankers and can get bacterial fireblight. The American species seems more resistant to disease and is better suited to a smaller site. Often we tend to favor trees from far away while those that grow among us are ignored.

LITTLELEAF LINDEN

Tilia cordata

To stand beneath a linden tree in summer bloom is a fragrant treat as fine as any rose could give, a garden's fleeting gift, vanishing into memory on a balmy breeze. The tree is stately and refined and doesn't straggle, bend or sprawl. In many ways its form is like its leaf, which is wider at the base and slowly tapers to the top.

There are many excellent lindens from which to choose. Our native tree, the American linden or basswood (*Tilia americana*), is very tall with larger leaves than the European types. Unfortunately, the native tree is difficult to find in garden centers. Another choice is the silver linden (*Tilia tomentosa*), with whitish hairs on the undersides of its leaves, but it too is difficult to find. The littleleaf linden is a staple of the nursery trade and rightly so. The tree is hardy even in the coldest sites and is rarely touched by disease or insect attack. Its moderate height makes it useful for the average lawn and its ability to withstand salt and dust has endeared it to urban growers everywhere. It's a tough resilient tree for modern times.

Some seedlings of this tree throw up suckers at the base, particularly if the tree is pruned hard or injured on the top. If the suckers are pruned but small stubs left, new buds will form and grow until the bottom of the tree looks like a gnarly burl with stiff brown spikes. If your tree sends up shoots, carefully trim them to the stem using a sharp, thin knife. Watch for buds that form on the edges of the cut and rub them off before they start to grow. If this is done carefully, the scars will heal and more shoots will not form. The grafted forms of linden rarely sucker but watch for any suckers from the rootstock below the graft. Varieties such as 'Glenleven' and 'Greenspire' will form uniform trees with little or no suckering on their stems. Even if they do send out suckers, any attention you need to give them will be more than repaid as your linden grows and blossoms in your garden.

STAGHORN SUMAC

Rhus typhina

Winter has arrived and you linger in the garden. The sun has set, the moon just risen. The stars of Orion sparkle in the eastern sky. The staghorn sumac's berries, fuzzy rubies in the light of day, are silhouetted cones atop the coarse, dark lines of branches. Three months later, the sun has set and still the air is cold, but Orion now lies in the western sky, and as sure as Earth still spins around the sun, another spring is on the way. The silhouettes of sumac berries still stand against the moon.

This plant is a delight at any time of year. The furry branches of the sumac in the spring might be racks of giant antlers standing on the garden floor. As you walk into a grouping on a summer's day, the shade is different from the ash or oak or linden tree's. The mood here fits a grove of palms, transplanted from their southern home. Already pyramids of flowers, yellow-green, terminate each velvet branch. In another month or two, when frost is the rule, the splendor of the rich red leaves, stitched with orange, will be among the garden's treasured sights.

The sumac's native sites are those with loose and stony soil, yet oddly, it often can be found in swamps. Its suckers expand into groups as large as space allows and will cover banks and places far too dry or poor for other plants. In a planting bed, you must remove the frequent suckers if you wish to keep this plant in check. If they are in the lawn just mow over them. A little pruning in the grove, a little path to wander through and you'll be richer, winter, summer, spring and fall.

Varieties

CUTLEAF SUMAC
Rhus typhina 'Laciniata'

The complex web of genes that guides the growth of every living thing can sometimes change when a random particle or wave or other happenstance creates an alteration. An upright tree can throw a seed whose limbs will never climb. A yellow stripe can form on leaves once only green. The cutleaf sumac's alteration looks planned by some elusive seamstress. As if creating lace, genetic knives have cut each leaflet of the compound leaves. The sun upon the garden floor makes points of light that dance with every breeze. As if this tampering with leaves was not enough, the painters had a good day too, for the more common reddish hues of sumac leaves in fall have been covered by a coat of cheerful yellow-orange. Even though you are too poor to own a landscape painting by Monet, a cutleaf sumac on your lawn will do as well.

JAPANESE TREE LILAC

Syringa reticula

For centuries the Goldi peoples in the valley of the Amur River in Manchuria knew the ivory blooms of the tree they called furagda. They smelled its honeyed perfume. Perhaps the children paused along the trail to stroke its smooth and lustrous bark. No doubt they listened to the rattle of the old seed pods when winter winds shook the smallish tree. Then a hundred years or so ago, groups of Europeans came. After collecting the furagda's seed, they traveled home, claiming another "discovery."

Though the Goldi must find the term "discovery" amusing, it is true that without the European and American plant explorers who combed the hills and valleys of Asia, we would not have many fine plants in our gardens today, including the Japanese tree lilac. This tough and showy tree is one of many trees and shrubs that have lately changed the look of northern gardens. With its shiny bark and vase-like form, this tree can fill a space in much the way the flowering cherries do in warmer sites. Its creamy yellow flowers are later than the other lilacs, extending even further the flowering season of this useful group of plants. What gives this tree an edge is its sheer tenacity. Resilient in the face of smog and car exhaust, the Japanese tree lilac is quickly filling an important role in urban scapes. The small size of the tree and its many attributes make it a first-class choice for any garden, whether surrounded by streets or fields and woods.

This tree will grow with little care, but much prefers a soil sweetened with lime and a rich loam. Those who feel an urge to prune can form its many arching stems into shapes that please them. If you relinquish the later seeds by pruning off the wilted flower heads, you will be rewarded by even more sweet flowers the following spring.

3

Conifers

WHEN A SOFT LIGHT SNOW SETTLES ON THE BRANCHES OF A BARREN TREE, it makes a color scheme of whites and grays. When snow festoons the evergreens, it makes a crystal crown for needled wreaths in every hue of green. The gardener of the north spends many days staring out the window, soaking in the light, cocooned against the cold, restless in the wait for spring. The conifers in winter glow with the warmth of living green, a welcome sight through a frosted window. When their swollen buds open in the spring, they're in their glory, fresh new needles glistening in the sun, the many colors of the garden's flowers emblazoned against a perfect foil.

When you plant a garden, plant some conifers. They occupy their site more solidly than most. Like verdant islands, they define the garden space. You will never tire of the wonders offered by this treasured group of plants.

JUNIPERS

Juniperus species

Junipers are commonly used ornamental plants. The varieties you see in the landscape have been chosen from species that grow in various climates around the world. They come in a range of sizes from tall upright trees to spreading shrubs and low ground covers. This large array of forms makes them suitable for numerous situations in the landscape. While this diversity is of great benefit to gardeners, it also creates problems because, while most junipers are fairly hardy, not all perform well in northern climates. If you live in a cold area, you need to be very selective in your choice of varieties. The majority of extremely hardy junipers come from two important species – *Juniperus horizontalis* and *Juniperus Sabina*. These are low- and moderately low-growing species respectively.

Junipers come from a wide range of habitats. It is, therefore, of the utmost importance to choose your varieties carefully. Planted in climates that are too damp or too cold, many varieties will be plagued with fungal diseases, many of which occur as secondary infections after winter damage has weakened or destroyed tissue. Find out which species do well in your area and which varieties within those species are most suited to what you are trying to accomplish in your garden plan.

Even when you have chosen your variety with care, a little cultural advice can help you create exceptional specimens. Each spring give your junipers a manicure. This involves combing out dead needles, which result from the normal dying of the three-year-old needles. Wearing a long-sleeved shirt and a pair of gloves, fluff the foliage vigorously, brushing with the direction of growth so that you don't break branches. Snow and ice can also do damage, breaking small or large limbs. Many upright specimens are particularly prone to such breakage, especially if they are situated under a house's eaves. Any broken branches should be pruned off cleanly to the first good limb. A simple measure that can save many an upright juniper is to gently bind the plant in the fall with stout twine in a spiral manner. Even hardy junipers may suffer some winter-damaged foliage. Using your pruning shears, cut out any damaged growth. Low spreading junipers need to have the accumulated clutter of fallen leaves and twigs combed out of them. If this material is left on the plants, the covered sections will die, for juniper foliage needs high-intensity light to survive.

Neglected junipers are all too common in the landscape. Their ratty appearance has turned many gardeners away from this fascinating group of plants, but with the proper choice of variety and a little extra attention each spring, you can create magnificent specimens that will become important anchor plants in your garden.

Virtually all junipers require well-drained soil in order to thrive. Avoid heavy, damp clay soils. If you have no choice but to plant in a clay soil, be sure that water drains away from the roots. A mulch layer on top of clay soils will allow the roots to remain near the surface where oxygen levels are higher. Many junipers are quite tolerant of dry conditions, but for optimum growth they should not be allowed to be without water for long periods. One reason for the sorry state of so many foundation plantings of juniper is that they are often placed under the house eaves where rain cannot reach the roots. Although such junipers may survive, they will certainly not attain the stature you desire. Most junipers prefer a neutral soil. Have your soil tested. If the pH is below 6.0, add lime to adjust the pH upwards. If your soil tests above 8.0 you should add sulfur to lower the pH.

Varieties

Ground Covers: Varieties Growing No Higher Than 1 ft. (30 cm)

CALGARY CARPET
Juniperus Sabina 'Calgary Carpet'

It is hard to say enough good things about this new variety. It satisfies every requirement for an exceptional low juniper. The foliage is soft and feathery, making it a joy to handle, in stark contrast to most junipers, which are so sharp-needled that gloves are a virtual necessity. The plant is uniformly circular in habit and very low. The new growth is a lovely lime green that matures to a dark, rich green. The needles are thin, adding to the soft and delicate texture of this beauty. Young plants grow somewhat slowly in comparison to most low varieties, but as the plant matures it becomes moderately vigorous. The northern origin of this variety (Calgary, Alberta, is a very cold city in winter) is testament to its hardiness. If well-grown, 'Calgary Carpet' does not suffer insect or disease problems. This gem is among the finest acquisitions you could make for your garden.

JAPANESE GARDEN JUNIPER
Juniperus procumbens 'Nana'

It is amusing and ironic that we in North America have found a way to mass-produce "instant" bonsai. This ancient Japanese art involves carefully training plants to become miniature reflections of larger landscapes. The process takes great patience, pruning skill and an understanding of the needs of a plant that is being constantly stressed by root and top pruning. Some specimens of bonsai are handed down through generations of bonsai gardeners – some are nearly 500 years old. That means that these plants have been watered and tended every day since the late 1400s. It staggers the imagination.

The Japanese garden juniper has one of the most distinctive and fascinating growth patterns among junipers. Its small, tight, medium-green foliage and its relatively slow cascading growth habit make it an ideal rock garden specimen and also allow a skilled pruner to create beautiful "bonsai" in one or two years. This most beautiful and useful variety, although not hardy in the coldest sites, is hardy in sheltered areas of Zone 4.

WAUKEGAN
Juniperus horizontalis 'Douglasii'

This is a living carpet of exceptional beauty, blue-gray in summer, plum color in winter. It is among the lowest growing of the junipers and is utterly dependable. It laughs at winter's most horrific deeds and shows not the slightest hint of disease. 'Waukegan' forms a neat, creeping rug on the surface of a planting bed. Placed in a niche in a stone wall, its horizontal sweeping branches show off the sinuous branching habit and bark that make it a useful plant for the practitioner of bonsai. Young plants tend to wander in one direction, but once in the ground 'Waukegan' spreads in every direction and becomes a super-hardy ground cover.

YUKON BELLE
Juniperus horizontalis 'Yukon Belle'

This book is written with the northern gardener in mind, so here is a variety that I can recommend to any gardener who lives south of the permafrost. Its branches reach like tendrils across the ground, flowing over and around obstacles such as rocks and stumps. The foliage is deep steel blue in summer, more muted in winter. If you are seeking rock garden specimens that will flow in and among stones and taller plants, 'Yukon Belle' is highly recommended.

Ground Cover, Low: Varieties Growing No Higher Than 20 in. (50 cm)

ARCADIA
Juniperus Sabina 'Arcadia'

This deep green variety originated from seed collected in the Ural Mountains of Russia and is exceptionally hardy. Its pleasing layered form is quite low in stature, with deep green branches that cascade outward as they grow. The needles are narrow, giving 'Arcadia' a fine texture. As with so many of the *Sabina* varieties, 'Arcadia' is very healthy. With all these admirable qualities, I find it surprising that this variety is not grown more; it is ideally suited as a bed border or in groupings.

There are three seedlings selected from the same batch of seed that 'Arcadia' was chosen from. These are somewhat less commonly available, but are increasing in popularity and deserve to be grown more. 'Buffalo' is similar in form to 'Arcadia' but perhaps brighter green. 'Broadmoor' has a gray-green color, and 'Skandia' has gray-blue foliage. All are hardy and healthy plants.

Ground Cover, Medium: Varieties Growing No Higher Than 3 ft. (1 m)

BLUE DANUBE
Juniperus Sabina 'Blue Danube'

Standing at the foot of a 6 ft. (2 m) wide 'Blue Danube' renews your faith in the beauty and usefulness of junipers. This vigorous gray-blue spreader forms as perfect a specimen as you could wish. The branches, whose tips bend up, grow outward rapidly, yet this large plant never gets more than "thigh high." The new growth is relatively soft to the touch and is a picture of hardiness and health. This is a juniper that responds to a minimum of care with maximum results. It makes a superb foundation plant and is very effective in larger plantings, both as a single specimen and in combination with other plants. In the proper site, 'Blue Danube' is a superior juniper.

MINT JULEP
Juniperus × *media* 'Mint Julep'

So many of the hardier cultivars of juniper are shades of blue. This plant shouts "green." It is the most refreshing shade of bright green. Although growing at least waist high, 'Mint Julep' is basically a spreading plant. This hybrid has *Sabina* juniper in its blood, and its foliage and form show it. Many hardy junipers are *Sabina* varieties, and the background of 'Mint Julep' helps to make this a hardy plant. If you live in Zone 4 or colder, be sure to give 'Mint Julep' wind protection, for it will windburn in open, windy sites. Although too tender for Arctic sites, this juniper can be grown by many northern gardeners. Its color, form and disease resistance will make it a valuable addition to your plantings. This variety is also found under the name 'Seagreen' in the nursery trade.

Ground Cover, Tall: Varieties Growing Taller Than 6 ft. (2 m)

SWEDISH JUNIPER
Juniperus communis 'Suecica'

Very few upright junipers do well in Zone 4. Some popular varieties such as 'Skyrocket' are often damaged or even die above the snowline, resulting in plants that resemble tall rats' nests. Although not reliably hardy in Zone 3, Swedish juniper is one of the better varieties for most northern gardens. The form is narrowly columnar with a characteristic upper point. From a distance it appears nearly solid, so dense are its tiny green needles. Even if you never use a pruning tool, the plant looks as though a patient hand has painstakingly shorn it every year. Gloves are a must when handling this variety as those dense, small needles are very sharp.

WICHITA BLUE
Juniperus scopulorum 'Wichita Blue'

Plant explorers are rather rare individuals. Some seek the far hills of China or Siberia, while others roam the forests and fields of home. They are, as a rule, unknown to all but a few, yet their gatherings of seeds, cuttings and plants surround you every day along the streets, in parks, around houses and in your garden. One such explorer found an outstanding specimen of the Rocky Mountain juniper. The medium-sized conical tree was denser than the others, with an excellent silvery-blue color, so he took some cuttings to propagate the new find. Today nurseries across an entire continent grow this same tree, the tree we call 'Wichita Blue'.

When 'Wichita Blue' was selected, it may have been denser than most members of its species, but it was not the tight, sheared cones you will probably purchase at your local nursery. Nurseries have discovered that most people prefer to buy a plant that represents their image of its final shape, even if it's not the natural form for the young tree. If you want this tree to appear as it did when it was first found, just let it go. It will turn into a handsome, dense tree with a lacy texture. If you want a controlled, tight shape, then you must keep up the shearing, or your plant will break out of its shell and try to assume its natural form.

With so few hardy upright junipers available, Rocky Mountain juniper has become increasingly popular in the landscape. In contrast to most juniper species, the Rocky Mountain junipers grow better in heavier soils. A poor performance by these junipers can often be traced back to the soil in which they are planted. Most varieties have been selected for their blue foliage, although the species is more often green or blue-green. Some other varieties that have proven hardy at least into Zone 4 are 'Blue Heaven', often called 'Blue Haven', 'Moonglow' and 'Pathfinder', a strikingly blue variety.

AMERICAN LARCH / TAMARACK / HACKMATACK

Larix laricina

The northern forest's last bright color show before the snow arrives is a golden grove of larch reflecting a setting sun. By then the maple's leaves are brown and lie freezing on the ground. Inside the grove at noon, the reflections off the yellow needles, on the ground and in the tree, create a mellow light that will not be seen again till spring.

Looking up into the branches of the larch in winter, one might imagine having found the "northern" ginkgo, its trunk a line from center Earth to outer space, its branches perpendicular. Yet every line is wavy, as if making up its mind were hard to do. The thin, short needles, indistinct from far away, give the tree a light and airy look. Romantics and Impressionists may weep.

Thomsen Blue Spruce, *Picea pungens* 'Thomsen' (p. 58)

Thume Blue Spruce, *Picea pungens* 'Thume' (p. 58)

Bristlecone Pine, *Pinus aristata* (p. 59)

Mugo Pine, *Pinus Mugo* (p. 59)

Brandon Cedar, *Thuja occidentalis* 'Brandon' (p. 61)

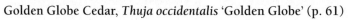

Golden Globe Cedar, *Thuja occidentalis* 'Golden Globe' (p. 61)

Holmstrup Cedar, *Thuja occidentalis* 'Holmstruppi' (p. 62)

(foreground) Little Giant Cedar, *Thuja occidentalis* 'Little Giant' (p. 62)

Nigra Cedar, *Thuja occidentalis* 'Nigra' (p. 62)

Unicorn Cedar, *Thuja occidentalis* 'Unicorn' (p. 63)

Smaragd Cedar, *Thuja occidentalis* 'Smaragd' (p. 63)

Sunkist Cedar, *Thuja occidentalis* 'Sunkist' (p. 63)

Cole's Prostrate Hemlock, *Tsuga canadensis* 'Cole's Prostrate' (p. 64)

Minima Hemlock, *Tsuga canadensis* 'Minima' (p. 65)

Flowering Shrubs

Northern Gold Forsythia, *Forsythia × ovata* 'Northern Gold' (p. 67)

Burning Bush, *Euonymus alata* (p. 66)

Virginal Mock Orange, *Philadelphus × virginalis* (p. 68)

Dart's Gold Ninebark, *Physocarpus opulifolius* 'Dart's Gold' (p. 69)

Abbotswood Potentilla, *Potentilla fruticosa* 'Abbotswood' (p. 70)

Goldfinger Potentilla, *Potentilla fruticosa* 'Goldfinger' (p. 70)

Primrose Beauty Potentilla, *Potentilla fruticosa* 'Primrose Beauty' (p. 71)

Agnes Rose, *Rosa* 'Agnes' (p. 72)

Blanc Double de Coubert Rose,
Rosa 'Blanc Double de Coubert'
(p. 72)

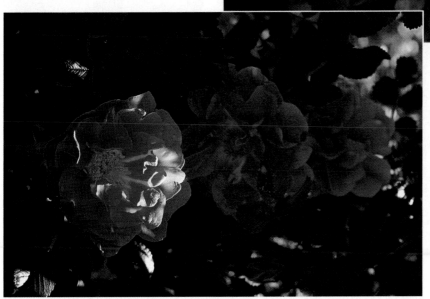

Jens Munk Rose, *Rosa* 'Jens Munk' (p. 72)

Königin Von Dänemark Rose, *Rosa*
'Königin Von Dänemark' (p. 72)

Quadra Rose, *Rosa* 'Quadra' (p. 72)

Stanwell Perpetual Rose, *Rosa* 'Stanwell Perpetual' (p. 73)

Thérèse Bugnet Rose, *Rosa* 'Thérèse Bugnet' (p. 73)

William Baffin Rose, *Rosa* 'William Baffin' (p. 73)

The wild larch nearly always grows just above a swamp or dampish place, but is at home in a well-drained soil as well. It is a forest tree and will need space, but in the open sun it may be somewhat squat, with a crown that is more twisted than a crowded larch.

The Japanese and European larches are also staples in the nursery trade, and both can be successful in Zone 3, but the native larch can be grown as far north as most of us will ever see. It can vary in its form and shape, with many being semi-weeping, others squat. Those who gather and disperse oddities from the woods have brought us dwarf forms of the larch, propagated from the dense masses of growth called witches' brooms that are found on the occasional tree, as well as other wild shapes that chance has landed in their path. If you seek these unusual forms, they can be found in specialty nurseries, but are rare.

NORWAY SPRUCE

Picea Abies

If you were to walk the Black Forest of Germany or trudge up the sides of the Alps in Switzerland, Italy, France or Austria, the evergreen you would see most would be the Norway spruce. Its tall narrow form, graceful sweeping branches and gray bark are a common sight throughout Europe. This elegant tree is now at home in many North American gardens. More often than not, however, the tree will be one of the numerous varieties that have been selected from the species. Indeed, no other conifer species can boast such a vast array of forms as the Norway spruce, among them tiny dwarfs, weeping forms, narrow uprights and varieties whose branches resemble snakes.

This species is a treasure trove to the northern gardener, for virtually all its forms are hardy in Zone 4, and many into areas far colder. The tremendous diversity of size, form, color and texture offer limitless design potential. Although many of these varieties were somewhat rare in the past, the increasing sophistication of the gardening public has created a demand for such material, and the nursery business has responded by making many more varieties available.

The Norway spruce is relatively undemanding. As long as it is well-drained and has a slightly acidic soil, it will prosper. As always, a loam rich in organics and with a mulch cover will promote optimum growth. The needles of most varieties withstand wind quite well, but in sites that act as wind tunnels you may get some yellowing in the winter, particularly in dry soils or where temperatures dip below -31°F (-35°C), but they generally bounce back with a new covering of rich green needles.

Varieties

NEST SPRUCE
Picea Abies 'Nidiformis'

Once while I was doing some landscaping, the owner asked me to remove the "scruffy little plant" at the entrance. There in the shadow of a Mugo pine, which now towered over it, was the sad remnant of a small spruce. Upon closer inspection, this hapless victim of improper plant placement turned out to be a nest spruce. Any sane landscaper would have thrown out the ragged remains, but I sensed possibilities.

Accompanied by howls of laughter from the crew, it was thrown on the truck and eventually ended up in the display garden. There I pruned off all the dead branches, which was most of the plant, and fine-pruned out the dead branchlets on what remained. It took two years or so before the plant began to take shape, but what emerged was an engaging specimen reminiscent of a Japanese bonsai pruned to resemble clouds sailing across the sky. I have been too lazy lately to carry on my pruning work, so now, 10 years after this waif was given its new home, its clouds have thickened into the characteristic form of the nest spruce, a spreading cushion of deep green with a depressed center, a nest for a discriminating evergreen bird.

Although called a dwarf, the nest spruce can eventually grow into a good-sized plant but will remain much wider than high. The low center usually remains, although this may become less noticeable with time. I do not know of any census of dwarf evergreens, but I would wager that this variety is the most popular low-growing form of all.

LITTLE GEM
Picea Abies 'Little Gem'

Many of our dwarf conifers originated as witches' brooms. The witches' broom is a spontaneous mutation that occurs with surprising frequency in conifers. During the rapid growth of a terminal bud, a cell's genetic information becomes altered. The normal growth pattern changes and the new growth is composed of relatively short and congested branchlets. If you train your eye to look for them, you will soon begin to notice these dense balls of growth on the occasional tree, most often at the top or on the end of a branch. If you take a piece of one of these witches' brooms and root it or graft it to a rootstock, you will maintain its dense globular habit.

'Little Gem' has its origins as a witches' broom that formed on the dwarf nest spruce. As you might expect, this dwarf mutation of a dwarf form is a very small plant indeed. It grows into a slightly flattened mound of tiny branchlets covered in very short, thin needles. Although a well-maintained plant will remain relatively uniform, 'Little Gem', as it ages, becomes just irregular enough to give it character deserving of a choice site in the garden. Be sure to keep it regularly groomed so that weeds or debris do not block its light. Failure to do so will result in dead patches that will not fill in quickly. Be attentive to this bristly little bun and it will delight you for many years.

OHLENDORFF
Picea Abies 'Ohlendorffii'

If you like your plants neat and tidy, here is a plant you'll treasure. As a young plant 'Ohlendorffii' is a tight, squat, conical form that looks as if it has been carefully sheared by an artist with a passion for geometry. It attains this perfection with no pruning whatsoever. As it grows upward, it becomes a neat, semi-dwarf, conical tree suitable for a small yard. There are several other dense pyramidal varieties that bear mentioning. 'Remontii' is very similar to 'Ohlendorffii', perhaps even tighter and smaller, but is a bit more difficult to find. Varieties that are somewhat more globular and lower growing are 'Diffusa', 'Compacta', 'Globosa Nana' and 'Microsperma'. All of these are very neat in habit and will satisfy those with a penchant for order.

WEEPING NORWAY SPRUCE
Picea Abies 'Farnsburg'

Most gardeners seem to either love or hate weeping trees. If you hate them, you'd best skip to the next variety, for this is as weepy as they come. The branches hang loosely down, with the very tips just slightly raised. If unstaked, this form will create a prostrate mat. It is most often staked when young so that the effect is of a dark green pillar whose sides and top flow back toward the ground. Weeping spruces were immensely popular at the turn of the century and are found in gardens throughout Europe. It was often planted in cemeteries, undoubtedly due to the obvious "sadness" of its nature. This would be an ideal plant to flow over the edges of a terrace wall, or to act as a verdant carpet for the floor of a large bed. We have highlighted a newer variety called 'Farnsburg', a selection from Switzerland, but the older, more common 'Inversa' is excellent, as is 'Frohburg' or 'Pendula Major'.

WHITE SPRUCE

Picea glauca

A row of dark green spruce separates two fields, seedlings planted long ago by squirrels and birds that sat upon a cedar fence, still visible where sweeping branches do not lie. These spruce are battered every year by heavy wind and blinding snow, and yet they stand so straight and tall you'd think the wind had let them be. These white spruce, or pasture spruce as they are often called, are common in abandoned fields, along the edge of woods and hugging shores where lesser trees would fail.

This is a spruce that grows from the Atlantic shore to the Rocky Mountains and north as far as gardens go. Its upward-arching branches, tightly packed in younger trees, make as fine a windbreak as you can plant. When grown alone, white spruce will form a tall, dense cone, most often darkly green but sometimes with a bluish tint.

This spruce grows in sites with lots of sun, preferring soil that's somewhat moist. It grows in acidic soil but will grow in neutral soils and is even tolerant of salt – a most obliging evergreen, and one at home in the coldest garden.

Varieties

DWARF ALBERTA SPRUCE
Picea glauca albertiana 'Conica'

In his *Manual of Dwarf Conifers*, Humphrey Welch tells the story of the discovery of this famous variety. In 1904 two celebrated botanists, Alfred Rehder and J.G. Jack of the Arnold Arboretum, were on a trip into the Rocky Mountains of Alberta. Because their train was late, they decided to take a walk into the surrounding woods. There they found a group of four similar, but very unusual, seedlings. The small trees were conical and dense with fine short needles that gave the plants a soft and pillowed look. Excitedly they dug the plants and brought them back to the arboretum. What they had found was to change the face of ornamental gardening forever. It became the most popular variety of evergreen ever introduced, the dwarf Alberta spruce.

From afar, the cone-shaped form of the dwarf Alberta spruce looks as if its surface has been carpeted with lime-green moss. To see it is to want to touch it, and although the small, thin needles are not cotton-soft, they are softer than the average spruce's. Although growth is slow, this plant will eventually reach 6 ft. (2 m), and even more if conditions are ideal. If you plan to grow this tree, be sure you place it so it's well protected from the winds. Although it is quite hardy, the thinness of its needles causes them to dry and burn when hit by winter winds. A hot southern exposure can cause problems as well. The sun of late winter can stimulate growth too early. The needles, full of water, freeze as the sun sets and the needles die. If possible, plant your trees facing east and protected from the prevailing north and west winds.

The dwarf Alberta spruce is subject to attacks of the red spider mite but this problem can be prevented by making sure that the plant is never stressed from lack of water, especially in the heat of midsummer. Give this marvelous gem a moist loam soil and protect it from the drying winter wind, and it will reward you with the excitement those two botanists must have felt when their eyes first fell upon this wondrous quirk of nature.

Many varieties are now available that are mutations or seedlings of the original 'Conica'. These include 'Alberta Globe', which is smaller and rounder; 'Lilliput', a very dwarf round plant; and 'Laurin', a very dwarf and dense form of the original. There are also plants having the same texture of foliage, but blue in color. 'Sander's Blue' is a good representative of this group.

SERBIAN SPRUCE

Picea Omorika

Growing high in the Tara Mountains, in what was once known as Yugoslavia, are groves of a most unusual spruce. Tall and exceedingly narrow in habit, they soar like cathedral spires from the rocky forest floor, their short branches growing downward, but with tips slightly raised, a series of elegant arches. The contrast between the dark green of the upper portion of the needles and the two broad white bands on their undersides creates an effect that must be seen to be appreciated. Another ornamental feature of this once rare tree is the deep purple color of its seed cones, which develop at the top of the tree even on young plants.

Gerd Krüssmann in his encyclopedic *Manual of Cultivated Conifers* tells us that the very narrow specimens grow high in the mountains. In the lower altitudes, where the seed is more readily obtained, the trees are wider; most of the seedlings grown today are from the wider race. Even these wider specimens are still quite narrow and elegant.

Serbian spruce does particularly well in the cool northeastern sections of North America. It grows naturally on limestone outcrops, so if your garden's soil is acidic, be sure to add some lime to bring the soil toward neutral. Make sure the soil is well-drained. The Serbian spruce is hardy in Zone 4 but, in colder sites, try to situate it where it will have protection from winter winds that can burn the thin needles.

Varieties

DWARF SERBIAN SPRUCE
Picea Omorika 'Nana'

This is a delightful dwarf form of the Serbian spruce. It was found as a witches' broom in Holland and brought into cultivation in the 1930s. It is the most common dwarf form of Serbian spruce grown today. It forms an irregular plant, which in old age becomes more or less conical. Provide a site where you can observe this plant at close range, as the contrasting white bands on the needles are a fascinating highlight. A new variety, which stays even smaller, is 'Pimoko'. This selection is still relatively hard to find but is superior if you are looking for a small, low mound.

COLORADO SPRUCE

Picea pungens

Northern gardeners can never delight in the opening of the camellia flowers or wonder at the hanging trusses of wisteria, but the north is the land of the evergreen. Vast forests of conifers extend to the very northernmost limits of vegetation, creeping out even into the edges of the tundra as wind-blown, stunted shrubs. Many evergreens are good choices for the garden, but one of the most outstanding of all is the Colorado spruce. At home in the most northern of gardens, this tall stately tree, with its stiff horizontal branching, is valuable as a specimen, in groups, or as a thick hedge, impervious to wind and cold.

Most gardeners know the Colorado spruce as the blue spruce because of the blue-green color of its needles. Hugging the edges of the Grand Canyon, stands of Colorado spruce were discovered that were very blue, and seed from such sources is now used to produce seedlings with good blue color. Over the last century, particularly outstanding blue seedlings have been discovered and propagated by grafting a shoot of the tree to a seedling rootstock. The difference between seedling blue spruce and grafted blue spruce has been the cause of misunderstanding, disappointment and even deception in the plant business. Many is the customer who has ordered a "blue spruce" from a nursery catalog. The customer, envisioning a shining silvery blue tree, is usually disappointed when the seedling shipped turns out to be green or blue-green at best. To make matters worse, when the customer goes to the local garden center, he or she is sold a product, usually aluminum sulfate, having been told that adding this powder to the soil will make the tree turn blue. This can lead to a second round of disappointment because the seedling can never be as blue as the grafted specimens the customer had in mind.

The color of the blue spruce is caused by a powder that is formed on the outside of the needles. If you rub a needle, it will become green. The rains of summer, and particularly the snow and ice of winter, gradually wear away the powder, and it is not till the new growth expands in spring that the spectacular blue mantle is renewed. Even the very best blue spruce will look duller by the end of winter. Iron is very important in the formation of the blue powder. In alkaline soils (high pH) the iron becomes chemically bound up with other elements and is unavailable to the tree. An acidifier such as aluminum sulfate or sulfur will change the chemistry of such soils, freeing iron, and enabling the tree to produce more powder. Most often, however, it is not the soil's chemistry that keeps the tree from turning blue, but the fact that it is a green or blue-green seedling, and no amount of any substance will change its color to blue. It is a case of knowing what you are buying.

The Colorado spruce is quite tolerant of different soil types, growing well in either sandy or clay soils, but it is very important to have good drainage, for it will not survive if the roots have to sit in water. Give your trees an annual feeding and keep them mulched when young to prevent competition from weeds. Keep your soil slightly acidic. The Colorado spruce will do well even in unprotected sites and is a good choice where wind rules out planting other species.

There are many varieties of blue spruce, and most have been chosen for their intense blue color. The majority of these selections are tall trees. Some of the better known varieties are 'Hoopsii', 'Koster', 'Moerheimii', 'Oldenburg' and the humorously named 'Fat Albert'. There are also many semi-dwarf and dwarf varieties available, and these are good choices for smaller gardens where the larger trees would soon outgrow their space.

Varieties

ISELI FASTIGIATA
Picea pungens 'Iseli Fastigiata'

It often takes decades or longer for a new variety to become established in the horticultural world. With such a tremendous selection already available, a new variety must have characteristics that set it apart from existing material. 'Iseli Fastigiata' is such a newcomer. Its stiff vertical branches are densely packed into a columnar form unique in the blue spruces. Although you may use this outstanding cultivar as a specimen, its architectural nature begs the designer to imagine curving rows of living blue pillars, geometrically precise arrangements reminiscent of a formal French garden or perhaps a vista to rival the cypress-studded hills of the Mediterranean. Plants such as 'Iseli Fastigiata' help us break the existing limitations of our northern gardens. Only your imagination sets the limits.

THOMSEN
Picea pungens 'Thomsen'

While driving along a back road in Maryland, I came upon an immense yard planted with dozens of holly trees, each one obviously a different variety. I could not bear to pass up such a garden. When the owner realized I was interested in his collection, he lost no time in giving me a detailed tour of his estate. After showing me his impressive holly groves, he led me behind the house where he had assembled the most comprehensive collection of blue spruce cultivars I had ever seen. Many specimens were 30 ft. (10 m) high or more, so the full splendor of these trees could be appreciated. After showing me most of them, he led me to a slightly younger tree and said, with a mixture of reverence and awe, "This is the best. It glows in the moonlight as if phosphorescent." I have never forgotten that moment as we gazed upward at the horizontal tiers of branches clothed in ethereal powder-blue needles. I vowed to find and propagate this bluest of blue spruce. As I look down the nursery rows of 'Thomsen' blue spruce today, I am elated to think that soon these same trees will be standing in gardens whose owners will be able to walk out in the full moon and witness the magic of this sapphire star.

THUME
Picea pungens 'Thume'

There are a host of excellent dwarf blue spruce varieties available. The most common is 'Glauca Globosa', often simply called dwarf blue spruce. This white-blue form is round in youth, gradually becoming conical with age. It is a lovely plant. There are others such as 'Montgomery', a similar but darker colored selection. 'St. Mary's Broom', propagated from a witches' broom, is a good choice if you are looking for a tiny plant.

One of the choicest cultivars is only now becoming known. The conical form of 'Thume' is uniform and dense, with a definite terminal, the image of an older tree in miniature. The color of this perfect little tree is silver-blue. Like other "dwarfs," this tree will someday grow to be as tall as the gardener, so give it space or plant material around it that can be removed.

BRISTLECONE PINE

Pinus aristata

Growing on a windswept mountain in Nevada are the oldest trees on Earth. When the sun glinted off the polished marble faces of the Egyptian pyramids and Stonehenge was still an empty plain, these same bristlecone pines were in their prime. It is staggering that these plants have endured 5000 years of drought, bitter winter winds, insects, disease and the other ravages of nature that eventually destroy all living things.

You may not be able to provide the unique habitat of that Nevada mountainside, but you should have little problem growing these fascinating pines. Although their native site is cool and somewhat dry, these adaptable pines are at home in nearly any site. They grow as irregular, open-branched trees with new growth that resembles long green shaving brushes. If you examine the needles closely, you will notice small white spots of resin that you could mistake for a small cluster of aphids.

It is essential that you plant the bristlecones in a perfectly drained soil. They prefer a loose gravelly soil. They are not heavy feeders so a rich soil is not necessary. Be sure the pH level of the soil is near neutral or slightly alkaline. They will not do well in acidic soils. If you can provide these conditions, you need only patience.

MUGO PINE

Pinus Mugo

Texture is an essential element of gardens. The graceful arches of ornamental grass, the pointed spikes of iris, the gossamer clouds of baby's breath, these textures elicit feelings in the viewer and can be used to direct the eye by their geometry. Pines, with their long needles, have a special texture, as if nature had frozen thousands of bursting green fireworks and artfully arranged them on stems. In spring the new growth decorates the trees with multitudes of ascending candles, adding yet another textural dimension to the garden. The Mugo pine, with its low stature and dense, dark green foliage, is one of the more useful and popular pines in modern gardens. It has special importance to us because of its unparalleled hardiness. This pine lives on the high Alps of Europe, among the rocks of the mountainsides, where winter winds are fierce and nearly ceaseless. Few plants are more adapted to growing in the north.

The Mugo pine has many forms. It is usually rather dense and round and eventually grows 10 to 13 ft. (3 to 4 m) in height. Occasionally a tree will grow quite tall, though this is less common. The form known as the pumilo Mugo pine (*Pinus Mugo* var. *pumilo*) is low and spreading, rarely growing more than 6 ft. (2 m) high, often lower. This form is well suited to smaller sites or places where too much height would be a problem. There are also numerous selections that offer a variety of forms, most of which are more dwarf than the species. Although they are still not common, more nurseries are carrying these selections.

This is a popular evergreen for shearing. Its relatively small annual growth and its naturally dense habit allow most any gardener to produce sculptured forms with relative ease. Nearly all nursery-grown specimens are sheared for several years when you buy them. The shearing process does, however, mask the growth habits of an individual seedling. They vary a great deal in vigor and form, and if you want plants that grow in a similar manner or if you want to choose a plant with a certain growth habit you should seek unpruned specimens. This is a case where a common nursery practice does not serve every gardener's needs.

If you plan on keeping your pines pruned, do your shearing in the early summer, after the new growth has expanded, but before the new terminal buds have set. It is usual to cut one-third to one-half of the candles. After being pruned, the cut end will form several buds for the next year's growth. Yearly pruning will keep the plant compact and very dense. Although many gardeners prune the Mugo pine into a bun shape, they can be molded into more complex forms.

Give your Mugo pine a well-drained soil, preferably one that is loose and airy. Although Mugo pines are tolerant of acid soils, a bit of lime may increase growth in naturally acid ground. A mulch of bark or needles will help keep weeds at bay, at the same time making more moisture available to the roots. With very little care, this rugged pine will keep your garden in fireworks all year long.

EASTERN WHITE CEDAR / ARBORVITAE

Thuja occidentalis

Our farm is bordered by a large cedar swamp. Several generations have labored putting a road through this bog so that they could work the fields on the other side. Yet it's doubtful any of these farmers would have wished the swamp away, for cedar is a priceless resource on a farm. There is no better wood for fence posts, and cedar boards provide the finest rot-free lumber available.

Besides producing valuable wood, eastern white cedar, and its horticultural varieties, provide some of the finest landscape material available for cold climates. Planted as a hedge, cedar creates a dense screening that looks good either pruned or natural. Tall, pyramidal varieties are used as accents in foundation plantings and to provide striking architectural elements in planting beds or screens. A variety of dwarf forms provides a wealth of evergreen material for sites where a small plant is needed.

Eastern white cedar, or more properly arborvitae, is a truly northern species with a natural range that extends well into the interior of eastern Canada. Although generally known as a swamp tree, cedar also grows in drier sites, especially where limestone is the bedrock. It is rarely found where the bedrock is volcanic, for these soils are often less fertile and usually quite acidic. It is a versatile tree, and with an understanding of its soil preferences most northern gardeners can grow this popular plant.

Foremost among the requirements of cedar is an adequate supply of moisture. This does not mean you must provide a swamp. Simply ensure that the soil does not dry out. A mulch layer will help keep moisture levels higher. Moisture is particularly important in the late fall prior to freeze-up. Cedars need this fall moisture to prevent their needles from drying in the cold winter wind. Those planted under house eaves or in dry gravelly ground will often lose their needles on the windward side. With adequate water, however, you can grow your cedars out in the open with few problems.

If your soil is acidic, be sure to lime the soil. If your soils are higher than a pH of 8, add sulfur to bring the level back toward neutral. If cedars receive enough water and if the soil's pH is near neutral, you should have little trouble growing these useful trees.

Each year cedars will cast off their third-year needles. In order to "freshen up" your plants in the late fall or early spring, comb out the dead foliage. A vigorous brushing with your arm will generally dislodge this material, at the same time letting you inhale the aromatic fragrance of the needles. If you intend on shearing your cedars, the optimum time for this operation is in early summer after the first flush of growth. If you prune during growth, more side buds will be stimulated to grow, and you will produce a denser plant. Cedars are very forgiving and can also be pruned in either spring or early fall with few ill effects on healthy plants. Be forewarned, however, that shearing tends to create a dense outer "shell" of foliage that is quite thin. Under this outer layer there will be little or no foliage. If the plant is ever damaged, a hole will result that can often be difficult to fill. One solution for such holes is to take some cotton twine and tie over a branch or two into the space, so that eventually the hole is filled. As with all hedging, be sure to keep the bottom of the plant wider than the top. If the bottom does not receive enough light, it will lose its foliage and look open and ragged.

Cedar is such a useful, hardy and healthy species, and there are so many good varieties available, choosing which varieties to highlight is a difficult task. The following provide a variety of forms that are relatively easy to locate in nurseries, but there are many other excellent cultivars available. Find out more about them and use them in your gardens.

Varieties

BRANDON
Thuja occidentalis 'Brandon'

The town of Brandon is located on the windswept Canadian prairie, a challenging locale for cedar. In this unlikely setting, a seedling was selected that could handle the dry cold of a plains winter and had the form and density of a first-class columnar variety. Although not as well known as many cedar varieties, 'Brandon' should be sought out by those living in similar, demanding winter conditions. Its deep green color, tight form, vigor and hardiness make it an outstanding selection.

GOLDEN GLOBE
Thuja occidentalis 'Golden Globe'

This globe cedar is similar to other globe types in all respects but color, which is a pleasing golden green in summer, intensifying during the fall and winter. Although many "gold" plants tend to have a sickly appearance, 'Golden Globe' looks vibrant and healthy. It provides an excellent color contrast in a planting bed, especially when combined with other evergreens.

HOLMSTRUP
Thuja occidentalis 'Holmstruppi'

This is a narrow, upright cedar with a pleasing combination of tightness of overall form, yet irregularity within that form. The base of 'Holmstrup' is rounded, the top narrowing to a sharp point. The individual twigs create a slightly twisted growth pattern. It is somewhat slower growing than many of the pyramidal varieties and useful in situations where a smaller plant is desirable.

LITTLE CHAMPION
Thuja occidentalis 'Little Champion'

Many "globe" cedars are sold without a variety name attached, but not all globes are created equal. There are differences in form, texture, vigor and color that often do not become apparent until the plant begins to mature. 'Little Champion' is distinctive because of its lacy texture. It is slightly wider than high and is notable for its ability to withstand heavy snow loads without breakage.

LITTLE GEM
Thuja occidentalis 'Little Gem'

In contrast to the geometric perfection of most other dwarf cedars, 'Little Gem' is irregular. It grows wider than high. In his book *Manual of Dwarf Conifers*, Humphrey J. Welch refers to the foliage looking "as though each little spray had been passed through a mangle." Those old enough to remember when wet clothes were passed through mangles, or wringers, will have a fair idea of the appearance of this unique cultivar.

LITTLE GIANT
Thuja occidentalis 'Little Giant'

This new Canadian introduction fills an important niche among the globe cedars. Most buyers of globe cedars see a small plant in a pot and think, "A perfect small plant for that little spot in my bed." In reality, many globe cedars grow to 6 ft. (2 m) or more. 'Little Giant' will rarely grow more than 2 ft. (60 cm) high. It is a very dense, round form, requiring little or no pruning to maintain its neat habit. The color is deep green and it maintains good color throughout winter. There are several other small globes that are more difficult to locate but bear mentioning because they are more dwarf than 'Little Giant'. In order of size from largest to smallest, they are 'Minima', 'Tiny Tim' and the rare but choice 'Rheindiana', which is the tiniest of all.

NIGRA
Thuja occidentalis 'Nigra'

Cedar is one of the most popular evergreen hedging materials. It is easy to shape, remains dense and is generally free of disease. Most cedar hedges are composed of seedlings, which are usually inexpensive but vary greatly in color, vigor and density. Many seedlings look rather drab in winter, a kind of brownish yellow-green. If you want to create a uniform hedge, use a vegetatively propagated variety – in other words, one that is propagated from cuttings rather than from seed. The variety 'Nigra' is one of the finest available for hedging. Those who took Latin in school will recognize nigra as meaning black, and the color of this selection is a very deep green. In winter 'Nigra' keeps its deep color. A hedge of this vigorous selection will satisfy the most demanding of gardeners. Another variety preferred by many growers is 'Techney'. It also keeps its deep green color in winter and forms a handsome specimen or hedge.

SMARAGD / EMERALD
Thuja occidentalis 'Smaragd'

Apparently English and American nurserymen didn't think we could pronounce the proper name of this new Danish sensation. Whether you call it 'Smaragd' or 'Emerald', this new pyramidal form is worth acquiring. The form of 'Smaragd' is quite unique. It is narrowly pyramidal, the base always slightly wider, the top having a characteristic long, sharp point. The foliage is much denser than most selections and, perhaps the most admirable of its qualities, stays a deep rich (yes, emerald) green in both summer and winter. It is also extremely hardy, performing well in very cold sites. Few new varieties have established themselves as quickly in the horticultural world as 'Smaragd' or have invoked more praise. It deserves it.

SUNKIST
Thuja occidentalis 'Sunkist'

Although there are several golden upright cedars, this relative newcomer outshines them all. Its dense, conical form is a golden-yellow color, with healthy foliage that is slightly wavy in appearance. In fall and winter, the color of this vigorous selection is a perfect complement to the greens of other conifers and, unless your winters are truly Arctic, 'Sunkist's' bright color will be untarnished by winter injury.

UNICORN
Thuja occidentalis 'Unicorn'

Because there are so few good narrow, upright evergreens available to northern gardeners, cedars occupy an exalted place among species, for there are many good upright cedars. Some of these grow a bit tall for use in foundation plantings but 'Unicorn' is a semi-dwarf upright that can be useful for a spot where height is limited. Its name is apt, for 'Unicorn' does resemble the horn of that mythical animal. It is very narrow and the foliage has a twisted spiral growth pattern. Let us hope your search for this cedar is more successful than the search for its namesake. Other slow-growing columnar forms worth locating are 'Malonyana', a tight, slim, tall tree; 'De Groot's Spire', a slow-growing thin spire; and 'Rosenthalii', an extremely slow-growing dark green column with dense short branchlets.

WOODWARDII
Thuja occidentalis 'Woodwardii'

Probably the most widely grown of the globe types, 'Woodwardii' forms a tight, rounded form that is slightly taller than wide. Its foliage is arranged in a characteristically radiating pattern from center to edge. It keeps a better color than most of the more vigorous globes. Although this is a dwarf form of cedar, be forewarned that globe types such as 'Little Champion' and 'Woodwardii' will eventually grow 6 ft. (2 m) high under good conditions.

CANADIAN HEMLOCK

Tsuga canadensis

Few evergreens are as stately as the hemlock. As a young tree, hemlock is a dense conical plant clothed in rich, dark green foliage. Older trees often attain immense stature, being one of the largest forest trees when allowed to escape the logger's saw. There is a grove of hemlocks in northwestern Connecticut called, ironically, Cathedral Pines. Sitting underneath these immense trees and realizing they have occupied that hillside for close to 300 years is an experience that leaves you with a respect and awe for the silent inhabitants of Earth.

The hemlock is found throughout eastern and western North America in cool, moist sites, often in shady glens where few other evergreens would thrive. Although the western hemlock (*Tsuga heterophylla*) and its forms are hardy into Zone 5, the species most suited to northern gardens is the eastern hemlock (*Tsuga canadensis*). What makes the hemlock doubly useful to the gardener is its ability to grow in either full sun or shade. The hemlock also makes a dense green hedge second to none.

If given the conditions it prefers, hemlock is a healthy tree. Hemlocks need a rich, moist, but well-drained loamy soil. They cannot be allowed to dry out, as moisture is critical to their well-being. Once established, a hemlock will grow in open sites if moisture is available; however, young transplants often dry out when exposed to drying winds without adequate water. Dry conditions are the number one reason for failure with hemlocks. Young plants will benefit from some shade, even if you must provide it with an artificial structure. As the plant grows older, such precautions are usually not necessary. Check your soil pH as well, for hemlocks prefer a slightly acidic soil.

In addition to the tree form, hemlocks come in an exciting array of dwarf forms, some of which are listed below. These allow you to choose just the right variety for your planting bed. Many of these varieties are difficult to find; however, a good selection is increasingly available and you should seek out hemlock cultivars to fill niches normally too shady for an evergreen, or where you want something special. Not all dwarf forms are hardy in the north. These are selections that are dependably hardy in Zone 4.

Varieties

COLE'S PROSTRATE
Tsuga canadensis 'Cole's Prostrate'

This is one of the lowest-growing hemlocks. It flows over the ground, rarely growing higher than 1 ft. (30 cm). The branch tops are exposed, with the branchlets curving downward. It looks picturesque growing among rocks or over a wall. It is slow growing, attaining a width of perhaps 3 ft. (1 m) in 15 or 20 years. Most plants of this variety, as with other dwarf hemlocks, are grafted onto seedling hemlocks, so the plant's growth rate will be somewhat dependent on the vigor of the rootstock. Although they are difficult to find, own-rooted plants will be smaller and even slower growing.

Be sure to give this plant some shade, as it does not thrive in open sun. It is suitable for growing in the filtered shade of larger trees if you ensure an adequate supply of water.

This variety originated in the White Mountains of New Hampshire and is very hardy.

JEDDELOH
Tsuga canadensis 'Jeddeloh'

This German variety grows as a dwarf shrub that arches outward, leaving the center of the plant slightly depressed, somewhat resembling a nest. The foliage is a rich, dark green. The plant is dense, seems at home in either sun or shade and is increasingly and deservedly popular.

MINIMA
Tsuga canadensis 'Minima'

This is a layered, arching shrub. The branches resemble wide green fans arranged in loose tiers. It rarely grows taller than 6 ft. (2 m) and becomes a plant of exceptional beauty. Its twiglets are very small, giving the bush an unusually dense texture. The variety 'Bennett' is virtually identical, and the two varieties have become mixed in the trade. Both are beautiful, but 'Minima' seems more resistant to sun and windburn in winter.

SARGENT'S WEEPING
Tsuga canadensis 'Sargentii'

In the late nineteenth century this weeping hemlock, called by one of its greatest promoters "a vernal fountain of eternal joy," took the horticultural world by storm. Soon gardens throughout Europe and America had specimens. For years the discovery of this hemlock, or more precisely four or five similar seedlings, was attributed to the famous American botanist Charles S. Sargent. In a book on the discovery of these hemlocks by Peter del Tredici, which reads like a horticultural detective story, a convincing case is made that, although the wealthy Sargent did introduce the tree, the discovery was probably made by a far-from-wealthy wanderer of the woods who dug and sold the original seedlings, which were found growing near each other. How many times in horticulture, as in other pursuits, do the accolades fall on the wrong shoulders?

4

Flowering Shrubs

WHEN YOU INHALE THE FRAGRANCE OF A FLOWER, YOU ARE PULLING A small number of molecules, so minuscule you cannot comprehend their size, into your sinuses; there they land on a tiny piece of tissue containing minute receptors that "smell" the combination of molecules unique to each flower.

The same brain that dispassionately analyzes this thing called a flower responds with emotions that are seemingly not the product of reason. When you see a flower, pleasant feelings follow. The smallest child and the oldest adult will have the same response. Our minds trigger the release of substances into our bloodstream that make viewing a flower a thing of joy. To many, the flower can calm turbulent emotions and turn sorrow to happiness. This is the primary reason that gardens are used by people for relaxation and the reason we give flowers to those we love or want to cheer. Perhaps someday we will surround and infuse our schools, our hospitals and our homes for the elderly with flowers. It's ironic that we spend untold amounts on gadgets that fill our homes and workplaces but consider it frivolous to spend a few dollars or a few minutes to decorate them with flowers, things that bring pleasure to us all.

BURNING BUSH

Euonymus alata

Plants use light to regulate their cycles. It is primarily light, or more specifically the number of daylight hours, that triggers a plant to begin or cease growth. The burning bush is a beacon that signals the change in light conditions. As the daylight hours wane in fall, leaves cease to make food and the green chlorophyll cells die. As they die, pigments in the cells, once masked by the green chlorophyll, become visible.

When this happens in the burning bush, leaves that in summer are a rich, dark green are transformed to fiery red. If the bush is growing in full sun the red will be more intense than one growing in partial shade. Soon the cells that connect the leaves to the stems wither and die. A gust of wind pops the leaves off their stems and returns them to the soil. The beacon fades until the next fall.

In addition to its fall color, the burning bush has another fascinating quirk. Its round, green stems have four brown corky ribs that run the length of each stem, broken only by the buds that are directly in line with the ribs. These ribs are probably an adaptation that helped protect the buds from damage. Whatever their use, they make burning bush, or as it is often called, cork wing euonymus, a fascinating plant to observe in any season. If you find these wings intriguing, you can even buy a variety called 'Monstrosa', which has unusually large cork wings. If you are looking for a lower-growing variety, 'Compacta' has all the attributes of the species but in a compact form.

Burning bush needs a bit of attention to grow to its potential. Be sure it has a rich loam soil, one with good drainage but also good water-holding ability. It needs a nearly neutral soil, so add lime where soils are acidic. Its white, fibrous roots are fairly shallow, so a good mulch cover will help keep them from winter's bite and will allow you to easily hand-weed them, preventing injury from cultivation tools. The euonymus is hardy in Zone 4, and can be grown in Zone 3 if the site is protected from wind. You should not see any serious diseases or insect problems in a well-grown bush.

NORTHERN GOLD FORSYTHIA

Forsythia × ovata 'Northern Gold'

Few sights in spring can cheer a winter-weary soul as much as the golden yellow blooms of a forsythia. Whether standing by itself or standing in a row, the bright four-petalled flowers on this bush herald spring in gardens everywhere, but those gardeners who live closer to the northern pole cannot grow the many types that fill more temperate gardens. The flower buds on most forsythias are often killed by low winter temperatures, except where buried by the snow. Even stems can die back in the coldest sites.

Recently several varieties have been bred using the early-flowering Korean forsythia (*Forsythia ovata*), which is a hardy and dependable bloomer. Among the very best is 'Northern Gold', a vigorous and upright grower with rich green healthy leaves that never appear scorched at their edges like some *ovata* hybrids. Just as the snow is leaving the garden, the petals of 'Northern Gold' unfold, beckoning you into the garden for another season.

Forsythias are relatively easy plants to grow. Give them good drainage, a moderately fertile soil whose pH is slightly acidic to neutral, keep them free of competition when young and they will grow into long-lasting bushes needing little care. Most forsythias eventually become large plants. If you wish to prune your forsythias, wait until just after flowering. If you prune before flowering, you will miss much of the show, as the forsythia blooms off the last year's wood. With a good pair of sharp shears or a pruning saw, cut off the older canes at ground level, leaving the newer canes. This will lower the height of your bush while maintaining its natural form. Flower buds will form on these new shoots for the next year's performance. If some thinning is done each year, you can maintain the plant without drastic shearing, but don't put off pruning because you're worried about hurting the bush. If it is healthy, it will rebound from pruning with incredible vigor. Of course, you can simply shear your bushes off at the desired height, but bear in mind this will leave many stubs and may invite in disease such as canker. Many people use the forsythia for a large hedge. Because of its vigorous nature, it is better suited to an informal hedge. If you are looking for a formal hedge, you may want to choose a less energetic subject. Another captivating new Korean forsythia hybrid, which is still rare, is an exceedingly hardy Canadian introduction called 'Happy Centennial'. It is a very dwarf plant, rarely growing more than 3 ft. (1 m) tall with profuse yellow blooms – a gem for the intrepid collector.

DECIDUOUS HOLLY / WINTERBERRY

Ilex verticillata

It is easy to spot the deciduous holly mixed among the somber grays and browns of fall and winter. The berries, closely set along the stems, hang tightly till found and eaten by birds. If you enjoy floral arrangements, the deciduous holly's stark brown stems and bright red fruit will be an added attraction. The dried berries keep their color and, even in the heat of a house, adhere to the stem for many months. There are many excellent selections available that bear large crops of showy berries, but be sure to include a lowly male or two, for without their flowers' pollen there is no fruit.

The deciduous holly grows in acid soils, often in a swamp or near a pond or stream. Where such conditions exist, it is often difficult to find a shrub that fits. Here is a plant to fill the bill. If you lack a wet spot, do not despair. As long as the soil is reasonably moist, you can grow the deciduous holly.

In summer the leaves are deep green, often with a subtle purple shading. Although it usually stays fairly small, a plant in a perfect situation may grow to 10 ft. (3 m). Though most of us in the north can never grow the hollies of Christmas lore, the deciduous holly can at least provide us with red winter berries to decorate our gardens and our homes.

VIRGINAL MOCK ORANGE

Philadelphus × virginalis

The thrusting light brown canes are dense and standing straight, their tips just slightly arched. The bush is plain, a loose and poorly tied straw broom forgotten till the spring. As you pass it every day, the simple leaves grow green, a robin's nest appears. Then when summer's warmth has settled in, five white petals open wide. Oh, what sweet delight, that scent upon the night!

It is hard not to wax poetic about the fragrance of this old favorite. Those who have been in an orange grove know the sweetness of the smell, but a grove of oranges overwhelms. The flowers of mock orange are sweet and yet restrained, a balance that will draw you every day to plunge your nose among the pure white blooms.

Give this plant a moist but well-drained loam, adding lime in acidic soil. If you wish to prune it, do it lightly, removing some of the older canes. It does not take kindly to a brutal pruning back.

Bridal-Wreath Spirea, *Spiraea* ×
Vanhouttei (p. 73)

Goldflame Spirea, *Spiraea Bumalda*
'Goldflame' (p. 74)

Little Princess Spirea, *Spiraea
japonica* 'Little Princess' (p. 74)

Goldmound Spirea, *Spiraea Bumalda* 'Goldmound' (p. 74)

Minuet Weigela, *Weigela* 'Minuet'
(p. 79)

Red Prince Weigela, *Weigela* 'Red Prince' (p. 79)

Tango Weigela, *Weigela* 'Tango' (p. 79)

Broadleaf Evergreens

Cliff-Green, *Paxistima Canbyi* (p. 80)

Golden Lights Azalea, *Rhododendron* 'Golden Lights' (p. 82)

Orchid Lights Azalea, *Rhododendron* 'Orchid Lights' (p. 83)

Rosy Lights Azalea, *Rhododendron* 'Rosy Lights' (p. 83)

Spicy Lights Azalea, *Rhododendron* 'Spicy Lights' (p. 83)

NINEBARK

Physocarpus opulifolius

It is little wonder that most gardeners are preoccupied with flowering bushes. Their blossoms are the jewels of the summer garden, bringing delight to the eye and often the nose as well. Generally overlooked, however, are the silhouettes of the winter garden. In winter the color and texture of your garden's dormant shrubs, often heightened by a backdrop of pure white snow, beckon the discerning eye. With careful selection and placement of shrubs, you can enhance the character of your winter garden, drawing the viewer in to delight in the subtler details of shrubs often overlooked or obscured by summer's luxuriance.

The ninebarks possess qualities that adorn the garden throughout the year. In the winter it is the bark that will draw you for a closer look. Curling off in delicate papery layers, the parchment-brown outer sheets expose the white inner bark as they pull away, a most unusual and beautiful effect. The popular golden form of ninebark blends its yellow tones with the many shades of green around it and the ninebark's white blossoms, although not as flashy as some, are nonetheless captivating. Even its pinkish seed clusters add a unique textural component in fall.

There is a dwarfer form of the popular golden ninebark called 'Dart's Gold'. Its foliage is a bright lemon yellow when in full sun, making it one of the finest yellow foliage plants for the north. Its small stature makes it useful in foundation plantings or in the shrub bed. It also forms a very showy low hedge.

This plant will demand little of you. Give it good drainage and a reasonably fertile soil and it will prosper. It does well even in open windy sites. The ninebarks will grow well in partial shade, but the yellow-leaved varieties need full sun to show off their color to best advantage. The ninebarks are a hardy and healthy group of plants. Remember them when you are wondering how to create interest in your winter garden.

POTENTILLA

Potentilla fruticosa

The flower of the potentilla is small and simple – five rounded petals surrounding a small center. Though the flower lacks the elegance of a multi-petaled rose or the extravagance of a hydrangea, it compensates with virtually unparalleled productivity. When the summer solstice is upon us, the potentillas begin their annual flowering marathon, ending only when the fall frosts shut them down. The attraction of potentilla does not end with its exuberant flowering. This is a plant of uncommon hardiness, flourishing even where winter temperatures drop to -40°F (-40°C) or lower. The small bird's-foot-shaped foliage is rarely damaged by insects, either. Potentillas are generally small shrubs, rarely growing more than 3 ft. (1 m) tall. This makes them very useful as foundation plants, for low hedges or for the shrub bed.

Potentillas will tolerate many garden soils, but to grow them to their potential, give them a neutral soil with good drainage and a fair amount of organic matter. Although drought tolerant, potentillas flower best when water is always available to them. As they mature, potentillas can become a bit straggly. Snow can also break them apart, destroying the neat form and density that most gardeners desire. You can shear younger plants each year by gathering up the branches together in your hands and pulling them upward into a tight mass. Take a sharp pair of pruning shears and cut off approximately half of the previous year's growth. The bush will spring back to a neat, rounded shape. This will also remove the previous year's flower heads, which hang on through winter into spring. As the bush ages, you may want to thin out some of the older branches to allow new, more vigorous shoots to take their place. A little annual attention will keep your potentillas in good form.

If you have an eye for the simple but an appetite for endless bloom, potentillas will give you what you seek.

Varieties

ABBOTSWOOD
Potentilla fruticosa 'Abbotswood'

Examine a blossom of 'Abbotswood' closely and you will see five glistening white petals. Step back and you will be looking at a thousand snowflakes resting on a mound of green. This is an outstanding variety whose first June flush of pure white flowers will leave you breathless and whose last flush in fall will be equalled only by drifts of winter snow.

FLOPPY DISC
Potentilla fruticosa 'Floppy Disc'

Ornamental plant breeders have many "holy grails" they are striving to find. A generation ago, a pure white marigold did not exist, but now they are commonplace. Breeders may be on the verge of producing a true blue rose, and with the introduction of 'Floppy Disc', we may finally have a pure pink potentilla. It is a serious risk to recommend a variety that is nearly as new as the ink on this page, but the flowers of this variety are a pink more intense than anything I have seen to date, and do not fade to ivory white in the summer as do most of the previously introduced pink varieties. Perhaps this is just a hint of the intensity of color we may see on future potentilla introductions. Seeing such color breakthroughs is always a thrill for the avid gardener.

'Floppy Disc' appears to be a profuse bloomer. Its color is most intense in the cooler temperatures and lower light levels of fall. The name may be less than romantic, but the sensuous hue of its blooms may lure even the most intense computer hacker from the keyboard.

GOLDFINGER
Potentilla fruticosa 'Goldfinger'

There are many excellent yellow-flowered potentillas. We have selected 'Goldfinger' for its large and brightly colored golden flowers, but also for its deep green foliage and clean appearance in fall, when many varieties seem somewhat muddled by old flower heads. 'Goldfinger' remains consistently showy throughout its flowering season, never failing to be covered with blossom. Other golden yellow varieties that bear mentioning are 'Coronation Triumph', 'Gold Drop', 'Goldstar', 'Jackmannii', 'Sutter's Gold' and 'Yellow Gem', a new low, spreading form.

PRIMROSE BEAUTY
Potentilla fruticosa 'Primrose Beauty'

The subtler tones of 'Primrose Beauty' will endear it to those who cherish pastels. The flowers are a soft yellow, the leaves a silvery green. Whether you wish to use this bush to contrast with the more vibrant colors of another, or to create a soft and dream-like quality to a corner of your garden, you will not regret your choice.

RED ACE
Potentilla fruticosa 'Red Ace'

Perhaps if this variety had not been named 'Red Ace', gardeners envisioning bright red flowers would not be disappointed when the first reddish-orange blossoms succumb to summer's intense light and heat and turn light yellow-orange. Maybe a name like 'Chameleon' would have been more appropriate. If we put preconceptions aside, this low, sprawling potentilla is a fascinating plant. The rising temperatures of summer and increasing daylight hours initiate changes in the amount of red pigment in the petals. The orange-red flowers of early summer become lighter with the warmth, then deeper again with the coolness of approaching fall, when this potentilla is at its best.

Unlike its more upright relatives, 'Red Ace' is low and sprawling with a finer branching structure. It is best used at the front of a bed. It is not quite as prolific as the upright potentillas, but does produce terrific early summer and fall flushes and sporadic late summer flowers. Although spurned by some because it does not live up to its name, 'Red Ace' is still a fascinating plant that can provide unique color and interest in your garden.

ROSES

Rosa species

We ask only that a rose bloom throughout the summer and fall, that its buds and flowers be plentiful and artfully arranged, with petals that reflect the scattered light in colors that are rare, that its perfume be so attractive we must detour every walk to visit and inhale, that its foliage be a paragon of health, that its stems be vigorous and green, even when the winter has been cold and without snow. So little to ask?

There are such roses. Not the tender teas that entice us with their perfect blooms, or the floribundas, grandifloras, miniatures and more, but the hardy shrubs, of which there are a goodly number. Modern breeding work has opened up a world of roses for the northern gardener.

Few flowers have as much to offer as the rose, but the cold-climate gardener is more likely to view the rose as an expensive annual because the varieties most often sold are tender. Roses are also associated with endless disease and insect problems, and indeed, many roses are plagued by such pests. But a careful sift of varieties will turn up shrubs that are as carefree as any plant can be. There is not space in such a book as this to do justice to the world of roses. Here are just a few selections to draw you in to the incredible diversity of roses, old and new. The shrub rose is not a single type of plant, but encompasses a range of texture, color and form that makes its culture more akin to discovering whole new groups of plants. You will not be disappointed by the hardy shrub roses.

Give your roses lots of sun and a moist but well-drained soil richly composted. Although many of the roses will perform in poorer soils, the rose will return your care with more flowers and better health.

Add lime to acidic soils, and if the summer turns dry, be sure to water before the plant is stressed so that growth is not interrupted or flowering slowed.

Varieties

AGNES
Rosa 'Agnes'

The delicate apricot tones of this rose represent one of the few yellows ever bred from the hardy *Rosa rugosa* species. Although it blooms only once in late spring, its intense fruity fragrance, delicate double blooms and dense, full form make it among the best yellow roses available for northern gardens.

BLANC DOUBLE DE COUBERT
Rosa 'Blanc Double de Coubert'

The 'Blanc' is a vigorous and spreading older *Rosa rugosa* hybrid that is extremely hardy. Its blooms are considered among the purest of whites and among the most fragrant. Established plants have good repeat bloom, particularly if the old flower heads are removed.

JENS MUNK
Rosa 'Jens Munk'

This is one of the newer Explorer roses from Canada. Its fragrant, semi-double blooms are a pure pink with no hint of mauve and appear in profusion till frost on super-hardy arching canes.

KÖNIGIN VON DÄNEMARK
Rosa 'Königin Von Dänemark'

This old representative of the *Rosa alba* group is quartered, meaning it has so many petals that they tend to divide into four sections. Its pure pink petals release an aroma that is intense and "expensive." It blooms during the summer and is hardy except in the very coldest sites.

QUADRA
Rosa 'Quadra'

A very new rose from Canada with a most exquisite double, deep red bloom. The canes are vigorous and hardy and will grow quite high. It is a very healthy rose that will bloom until the winter shuts it down.

STANWELL PERPETUAL
Rosa 'Stanwell Perpetual'

A chance seedling from England, 'Stanwell Perpetual' is continual blooming. Its hardy slender canes slowly mound to form a spreading, rounded bush. The delicate white double blooms are flushed with a touch of pink and smell as though distilled for elfin queens.

THÉRÈSE BUGNET
Rosa 'Thérèse Bugnet'

'Thérèse Bugnet' has a fragrant, double, soft-pink bloom whose deep red stems survive sub-arctic sites. The bush is tall and arching, a carefree shrub that is prolific in late spring and lightly repeats till frost.

WILLIAM BAFFIN
Rosa 'William Baffin'

This new pillar rose is a healthy bush that will reach a trellis top even where the winter's winds are cold and cruel. Its vibrant blooms are neon-pink and appear throughout the season.

SPIREA

Spiraea species

The spireas offer an entire rack of spices with which to season your garden. Few groups of plants are as diverse. Spireas vary from tall arching shrubs bedecked with long sprays of white flowers to dwarf mounds covered in pink blossoms as delicate as tiny parasols. With such a variation in form, texture and color, the spireas can be useful in many different applications within the garden.

Spireas are undemanding as garden subjects. Most need good drainage and a moderately fertile soil to prosper. They do well in somewhat acid soils, but benefit if limed. As with nearly any shrub, a regular program of composts and mulches improves growth considerably. The larger growing spireas need to be thinned regularly to maintain vigorous, healthy growth. Take out some of the older canes each spring. The more dwarf varieties will need an annual shearing to remove dead flower heads from the previous year and may need some thinning as they age.

The varieties below represent a sampling of the many different varieties available.

Varieties

BRIDAL-WREATH
Spiraea × *Vanhouttei*

Few shrubs have as many admirers as the bridal-wreath. In June the long, arching stems produce masses of flowers, each one tiny, but together making graceful sprays of purest white that are indelibly etched into the gardening psyche of the temperate world. Bridal-wreath makes an informal hedge of the first order and is useful as a background plant in larger beds. This spirea is often used in shady sites because of its tolerance of low light levels. Occasionally, thin out older canes. If you head back the branches, you will lose the graceful character of the arching branches.

GOLDFLAME
Spiraea Bumalda 'Goldflame'

Although endowed with pink flowers in summer, this small plant is first and foremost a foliage plant. In early spring the young foliage emerges a crimson red. As the shoots elongate, the leaves take on varied colors ranging from pink to yellow to green. Individual leaves may display the complete range of colors. All summer this plant is a multi-hued harlequin in the garden. Plant them in masses for a spectacular effect. In fall 'Goldflame' returns to the red end of the spectrum, giving a last bravo before the snows. Hardy in nearly every garden, this plant needs only a bit of shearing in spring to keep it tidy.

GOLDMOUND
Spiraea Bumalda 'Goldmound'

This is among the very smallest of spireas. 'Goldmound' is ideal for the rock garden or as an edging in a shrub bed. Its bright yellow foliage, infused with subtle hues of lime in light shade, brightens the garden all season. In summer a frosting of delicate pink flower clusters rime this diminutive gem. Shear lightly in early spring to remove the old flower clusters.

LITTLE PRINCESS
Spiraea japonica 'Little Princess'

The modern world is an urban world. Those living on city lots do not have the space necessary to grow many of the larger trees and shrubs. The demand for dwarf plants to satisfy the needs of small gardens has led to the introduction of many new selections. A superb example is 'Little Princess'. With its low growth habit and tidy form, this small plant is at home in the most compact of gardens. Its bright green foliage is attractive from early spring till late fall when it turns maroon red. 'Little Princess' is most attractive in July when clouds of pink blossoms lie like a summer haze on the branch tips. The delicate structure of this small plant belies a hardiness and tenacity rare in the plant world. It is a superb and useful plant for the northern garden.

LILAC

Syringa species

There are those of us who scramble over crumbling cellar holes in search of plants left by forgotten dwellers of abandoned farms. Sometimes a hop plant climbs a ragged remnant of an orchard, or a rose holds out against the forest edge, but the most common sentinel is a lilac, still tenaciously occupying the site where it was planted, perhaps a century before.

Hardiness and persistence have always been admired traits of the lilac, but it is the flower, and more particularly the flower's perfume, that has made it among the world's most treasured plants. It is said that the sense of smell is the strongest stimulus of memory. For many, the fragrance of the lilac stirs dreams of their past, perhaps even dreams of those very farms where once as children they played under the same bush whose perfume now floats among the wild raspberry and balsam.

Today there is a bewildering array of lilac species and a wealth of hybrids between the various species and within species. Flower colors from the deepest purples to the lightest pinks and blues tempt your senses. Lilacs of all shapes and sizes can be valuable additions to your garden designs. Nearly all of these species and hybrids are worthy garden subjects, but unless you have unlimited space, you should choose those lilacs that best fit your needs and desires. Whatever your choice, you will rarely be disappointed by the lilacs.

As a group, lilacs are relatively easy to grow. Most are hardy enough for northern gardens and, provided they are well-drained, they will grow in most soils. They prefer a neutral soil and will benefit from annual additions of compost.

Do not be impatient with newly set-out lilacs. It often takes several years for a lilac to produce flower buds. If you decide you should prune your lilacs, bear in mind that they form their flower buds on the terminals of the shoots. If you prune the stems, you will remove the flower buds. Unless you are trying to make a lilac hedge, it is better to thin out some of the branches in order to let more light into the center of the bush and encourage growth on the remaining branches. If you want to cut back the entire bush, do so in the spring, immediately following flowering. That way the new shoots will have a chance to form flower buds before fall. An alternative is to cut out the older, taller trunks and allow some of the new suckers to grow. Old sections of lilacs eventually become relatively unproductive. This process of rejuvenation will encourage new productive wood and will allow you to maintain the lilac at a reasonable height. You can also create picturesque specimens by pruning older lilac stems to enhance their character. As always, pruning is a tool to accomplish an end.

Many lilacs will sucker profusely. This may present a problem in certain planting sites. If you do not want to spend countless hours pulling unwanted shoots, plant your lilac where it can expand and flourish. If you need to keep a suckering lilac confined, pull any new suckers upward and back toward the center of the plant. Cut them off as close to the main roots as possible. Simply cutting the suckers at ground level will encourage several new suckers to appear just below the cut.

When lilacs are produced in the nursery, they may be propagated by seed or by cuttings or they may be grafted plants. Plants grown from seed or from cuttings grow on their own roots and, therefore, any new suckers will produce the same type of flowers as the existing stems. Many of the hybrid lilacs are produced by grafting the desired variety onto common lilac or onto such roots as green ash or privet. Be warned that a lilac grafted onto common lilac forms new shoots that will not have flowers of the same color or form and these new shoots need to be cut out to maintain the trueness of flower. Those grafted to ash or privet should be planted deeply so that the lilac part can form its own roots, because eventually the graft unions on such plants fail, and your lilac may snap off at the union. Your nurseryman should be able to tell you how your lilac was propagated so you can plant accordingly. With improved rooting techniques and new technologies such as tissue culture, grafting is becoming an outdated process, but many grafted plants are still on the market and the consumer must beware.

Species

CHINESE LILAC
Syringa × chinensis

A graceful shrub that grows both wide and high, the Chinese lilac's blowsy flower heads are pink with a subtle perfume. The form known as 'Saugeana' is a very fine plant. It is a species that has been too long in the wings – it deserves center stage.

DWARF KOREAN LILAC
Syringa patula

A relative newcomer to the horticultural scene, this small lilac has become very popular because of its suitability for low hedges and as small specimens. The most popular variety is 'Miss Kim'. Its pink-lavender flowers are profuse in spring after the other lilacs have finished, and a second lighter flowering is not uncommon in the fall. This species is probably too tender for areas colder than Zone 4. Be sure it is grown in a well-drained site, as it will not tolerate wet roots.

PRESTON HYBRIDS
Syringa × prestoniae

This group of hybrids has come to play an important role in northern gardens. Flowering just after the common lilacs, they allow you to extend the lilac season to nearly a month. Their vigor and hardiness are surpassed only by the delicate beauty of their immense diaphanous flower heads. You may also appreciate the fact that these plants do not sucker as profusely as the common lilac. Be warned, however, that they can become very large plants, capable of dwarfing a one-story house at maturity. Some of the most notable varieties are 'Donald Wyman', 'James Macfarlane' and 'Miss Canada', all various shades of pink.

COMMON LILAC
Syringa vulgaris

To be common is the finest compliment that we can pay in horticulture. The common lilac is one of the best known garden plants. It is a tenacious plant that spreads outward to occupy as much space as it is allowed and will outlast the best of us if given the care it deserves. Its flowers are tightly clustered and of legendary fragrance. In the last two centuries, breeders around the world have spent lifetimes developing a spectrum of colors that is truly beyond the scope of all but the most devoted of collectors. Lilacs come in shades of lilac, purple, red, blue, violet, pink, lavender, white and even one creamy yellow and a bicolor. There are far too many varieties to describe in a volume such as this, but the photograph will perhaps inspire you to seek out some of these enchanting plants.

LOWBUSH BLUEBERRY

Vaccinium angustifolium

There are very few people who don't love a blueberry pie or fresh blueberries with cream, but not many people think of the blueberry as a garden plant. A trip through the blueberry barrens of the northeast in the fall would quickly convince you that the blueberry has more to offer than taste. In autumn the small leaves turn to brilliant shades of red, often with a hint of orange. A bed of these dense, low shrubs in fall can add a swath of color to your garden equal in splendor to the burning bush or sugar maple.

Add to this the fact that the berries themselves are highly ornamental and you have a first-class garden plant. Lately the lowbush blueberry has been hybridized with the highbush blueberry (*Vaccinium corymbosum*) to produce a race of plants known as the half-highs. Many of these plants have maintained the deep fall coloration of their lowbush parent, yet have the berry size of the highbush parent. Some of the most ornamental lowbush varieties are 'North Country', 'North Sky' and 'Top Hat', a very dwarf plant that is excellent in the rock garden and a fine candidate for bonsai. Some excellent half-highs are 'St. Cloud', 'Friendship' and 'Northblue'.

The blueberry grows on acidic soils and will not prosper in a limed garden soil. Be sure your pH is no higher than 5.0 or your foliage will yellow and growth will be poor. As well, the ground must be perfectly drained. Many growers add organic matter such as rotted sawdust to the soil to provide the loose texture the delicate thin roots prefer. Here is a plant for sites where the soil is thin and poor. The lowbush blueberry is an undemanding plant and with a little care can become a colorful addition to your garden.

VIBURNUM

Viburnum species

In the dappled shade of the maple and beech stands a shrub decorated with starry white umbrellas as large as dessert plates. Later in the summer red-berried parasols tempt the passing birds to stay and feast, a wily ploy to spread the seed. A shrub with such features that grows in shade should be an honored guest in any garden, yet many gardeners know very little about viburnums. In warmer climes, the fragrant viburnums are better known, but in the north viburnums are still rarely grown. An increasing sophistication among gardeners, a better awareness of native plant material and a new selection of improved forms will help to make more gardeners aware of this spectacular and useful group of plants.

Viburnums are most often found growing in the understories of forests or at their edges. They prefer a moist loamy soil, something akin to the forest litter in which their musty-smelling roots roam naturally. They like a slightly acidic soil, but not as acid as the blueberry might prefer. Once established they will tolerate some drought, but don't plant them in a dry soil or they will never reach their full potential.

WILD RAISIN

Viburnum cassinoides

Driving along a country road, you might mistake this plant for a large-leaved rhododendron that has strayed from its southern home. Its thick, green leaves are only one of its many features. In early summer, large flat clusters of pure white flowers grow into deep red berries that turn purple-black and, as they dry, turn to "raisins," unless first found by birds. The wild raisin can be grown in sun or dappled shade and prefers moist, acidic ground. It's a perfect plant for a cool, damp, shady site where most shrubs will not live. It can grow quite tall if never pruned, so give it space. This native plant merits more attention and deserves work by amateur and professional selectors and breeders. Many forms that have larger flower clusters or compact forms could be brought into cultivation.

WAYFARING TREE

Viburnum Lantana

If you could shrink yourself to the size of a flea and be put on the underside of a wayfaring tree leaf, you would be dwarfed by long stalks called indentum. To the eye, and to the hand, these stalks give the leaf a woolly look and feel, a softness uncommon among garden plants. Such unusual textures add interest to the garden.

In early summer large umbrella-shaped flower heads cover the ends of the stiff stems. The large white flowers against the olive green leaves is a truly spectacular sight. These flowers become clusters of deepest red fruit as they mature, hanging on till winter if not found first by birds filling their bellies for the long trip south.

Although perfectly at home in full sun, this large shrub is a prime candidate for the shade garden, growing well in any but the darkest of sites. It prefers the moist leaf-mold of a forest floor, but you can provide such conditions in the midst of your garden with a mulch. Although it enjoys moisture, be sure its roots are not sitting in water.

Recent breeding has provided gardeners with a number of excellent new viburnum cultivars. Among these is 'Mohican', an outstanding selection of wayfaring tree that is rounded, full and very floriferous.

WEIGELA

Weigela species

Arriving with the belated warm touch of summer are the hummingbirds. Darting from flower to flower on seemingly translucent wings, they give immense pleasure to gardeners lucky enough to have them visit. These birds pollinate the more tubular flowers such as the honeysuckles, rhododendrons and weigelas. A large grouping of weigelas is a magnet for hummingbirds, satisfying their long searching tongues with nectar for many weeks. Not all weigelas are suitable for the northern garden, however. Varieties such as the old red 'Bristol Ruby', so long a mainstay of many gardens, is a disappointment in many colder regions. Each winter it dies back to near the ground, surviving only where snow covers its branches. Because it sends out new shoots and flowers on the new wood, people still plant this variety in the north, but there are many better weigelas for such sites.

Give your weigelas a sunny location with good drainage and compost your soil to keep the plants in prime condition. As the plant grows older, you may wish to reduce its height. By thinning out older growth, you can rejuvenate your shrub while keeping it a manageable size. If you have only a small space, look for some of the dwarfer varieties for it is difficult to maintain the vigorous varieties at a small size.

Varieties

MINUET
Weigela 'Minuet'

This is one of the "dance series" of weigelas bred by Agriculture Canada for hardiness and dwarf stature. In most gardens 'Minuet' will seldom exceed 3 ft. (1 m) in height and will maintain a compact globular form. Its profuse, deep pink blossoms appear for many weeks in early summer. Even when it's not in flower, the foliage is an attractive deep green with a blush of purple.

RED PRINCE
Weigela 'Red Prince'

A superstar among the weigelas, this very hardy plant covers itself in crimson red flowers. 'Red Prince' can flower over a period of six weeks and then have the odd flower in the fall. For sheer exuberance, purity of color, hardiness and vigor, this new introduction from Iowa is unmatched. Disease or insect problems are very rare, making this outstanding and very important new plant truly a prince.

TANGO
Weigela 'Tango'

This is a sleeper in the weigela world. Released as a member of the "dance series," it is as yet little known, but if you are searching for dwarf shrubs with character, seek out this slow-growing weigela. Its dense rounded form is covered in deep purple foliage and in bloom is graced by blooms of deepest pink.

5

Broadleaf Evergreens

AS ONE NEARS THE NORTH POLE, THE NUMBER OF SPECIES THAT KEEP THEIR leaves in winter dwindles rapidly. Once into areas where temperatures drop to -22°F (-30°C) most of the rhododendrons, boxwoods, hollies, firethorns, evergreen euonymus and mountain laurels are failures without special protection. Out of the vast numbers of broadleaf evergreens in the world, only a very few will survive a long and brutal winter.

Among these few are plants of exquisite rareness. Select varieties of rhododendron, denizen of forest floors and lionized by plant collectors everywhere, its showy blossoms lending lushness to the humblest of gardens, and the cliff-green, perhaps tucked into a special corner, are plants that await the adventurous. These special few are truly treasures to the man or woman who tends the soils of the north.

CLIFF-GREEN / MOUNTAIN-LOVER / RATSTRIPPER

Paxistima Canbyi

Imagine having a knot garden with tightly clipped miniature hedges of boxwood in your northern garden. What was once a pipe dream in the north can be a reality with cliff-green, for this plant, with its dwarf stature and tiny leaves of deepest green, can fill such niches in your garden much like the boxwood of more southerly regions. Cliff-green is a spreading plant and will, over time, cover large areas, making it an ideal candidate for a groundcover or edging. Where it extends beyond the bounds you have set for it, simply slice down with a spade and remove the shallow roots and stems.

Cliff-green was found clambering over rocky faces of the Appalachian Mountains. It appreciates a moist, well-drained soil but will tolerate short periods of drought. Its leathery leaves are well adapted for retaining moisture and fending off the drying effects of cold winters, but in the coldest sites, protect it from the wind. Give it a slightly acidic soil and a light mulch layer. This plant is hardy in Zone 4 and may survive in protected sites in Zone 3.

AZALEAS AND RHODODENDRONS

Rhododendron species

In winter you can gaze out your window and know how cold it is by the rhododendrons. When the temperature drops below freezing, the edges of their leaves start to curl downward. The colder it gets the more pronounced the curl. At -4°F (-20°C), the leaves have become thin tubes resembling drinking straws more than leaves. By exposing as little tissue as possible to the drying cold winds, the rhododendron leaves are able to survive temperatures that would destroy them if they remained flat, an amazing detail of evolutionary adaptation. It is with relief that we watch the dead-looking leaves unfurl again as the warmer air triggers them to relax. Several years ago northern gardeners may not have been able to see this process take place, for there were no varieties available for truly northern sites.

There are dozens of rhododendron species in cultivation, and literally thousands of varieties: some rhododendrons are diminutive ground-hugging plants, others grow into forest trees and every size in between. Sadly for the northern gardener, this vast range of rhododendron material is of little value. Our cold gardens do not offer most rhododendrons a very hospitable home. Low temperatures kill both flower and vegetative buds and the drying winter winds wither the leaves of most evergreen types. In the past, very few varieties existed that would survive the extremes of northern gardens, but the recent work of several breeders has changed this forever. A continually increasing number of very hardy rhododendrons is making its way into the marketplace and allowing northerners to experience the joys of this remarkable group of plants. Now we, like gardeners throughout the world, can revel in their spectacular flowers, which provide a veritable rainbow of colors.

Azaleas are grouped together with rhododendrons because botanically speaking, azaleas are rhododendrons. Although there are evergreen azaleas, for our purposes an azalea is simply a rhododendron that loses its leaves each year.

If you wish to grow these wonderful plants to perfection, a little cultural advice is in order. Rhododendrons prefer acidic soils, ranging in pH from 4 to 5.5. Be sure to have your soil tested and adjust your pH accordingly. No matter how much loving care you give them, most rhododendrons will not survive an alkaline soil. The iron, so necessary to their health, becomes chemically bound in such soils and they cannot function properly.

Soil texture is very important to rhododendrons. They need a soil with a high percentage of organic material to prosper. Work copious amounts of materials such as shredded bark, peat moss, leaves or pine needles into your planting soil. It is highly advisable to mulch your plants as well. The rhododendron has very fine roots that have difficulty penetrating heavy soils. Its delicate roots also make it imperative that you avoid cultivating deeply. Great damage can be done to a rhododendron by an over-zealous weeder with a hoe. A properly mulched rhododendron is easy to weed by hand.

Be sure that your rhodos don't dry out. Those fine roots will turn to dust if the soil loses its water. Lastly, most rhododendrons are at home in the understory of forests or at the edges of woods, so give them a site that receives a filtered light, or one that receives direct sun only part of the day. I find eastern exposures are ideal. A rhododendron placed in a hot sunny spot will usually be very unhappy. However, it is an interesting fact that many of the new hardy varieties have a greater tolerance to sun than most of the larger leaved, more tender varieties.

Rhododendrons are nearly always grown in containers at the nursery. When you are planting a rhododendron, examine the rootball when you unpot it. If the roots have formed a thick mat on the outside of the ball, trim these roots. There are several methods of doing this. Perhaps the easiest is simply to take a knife and make shallow vertical cuts from the top to the bottom of the ball several times around the outside of the ball. This will stimulate new roots to form so they will grow outward into the surrounding soil. If the mat is not too thick, you may be able to gently "comb" the roots to free them up. Some people simply take a knife and slice the outside mat completely off. It is imperative that a rootbound rhododendron be treated in one of these ways. If you do not trim the roots, they will rarely form a healthy outreaching root system, and your plant will gradually deteriorate.

Many rhododendrons and azaleas have a tendency to grow into rather tall, lanky plants. If you wish to keep your plant more compact, it is advisable to prune your plants when they are young. Soon after the new growth has commenced in spring, pinch off the terminals between your thumb and forefinger or with a pair of pruning shears. This will induce the shoot to send out several lateral shoots, thereby thickening the plant. Although you may initially sacrifice bloom, your plant in the future will be compact with more flower buds. This technique is useful on older plants as well.

In order to stimulate greater production of flower buds, it is advisable to pinch off the flowers after the petals have withered. This prevents seed from forming, saving energy for growth and stimulating the plant to set more flower buds that will open next spring. Be careful, however, that you do not injure the new shoots, which will just be starting to grow in a whorl directly under the flower.

Care and attention to details will help you establish these hardy rhododendrons. Once they are growing in your garden, a little annual care will be amply rewarded with flowers as enchanting as any garden can hope to grow.

Varieties

THE AZALEAS

GOLDEN LIGHTS
Rhododendron 'Golden Lights'

The recent introduction of a group of azaleas called the Northern Lights series has made a lasting impact on the quality of far northern gardens. These azaleas, bred in Minnesota, have extended the range of azaleas into Zone 3 and even into Zone 2 if adequate protection can be provided. Hardiness has not meant the sacrifice of beauty. 'Golden Lights' rivals the finest of the older golden yellow varieties. Even as a young plant, its large fragrant trusses are a beacon of color in gardens just entering the warm days of late spring. The foliage is deep green and amply covers this erect plant. Mildew, the disease so dreaded in many azaleas, rarely appears on this variety. This plant will repay any gold spent on it with golden petals far more precious and refined than yellow metal.

ORCHID LIGHTS
Rhododendron 'Orchid Lights'

This is probably the hardiest cultivated azalea you can grow. It is a compact, dense plant, covered with masses of small orchid-pink blossoms in spring. The low stature of 'Orchid Lights' makes it an ideal choice for a site where many azaleas would prove too large, such as a rock garden or a perennial border. The appearance of this azalea, with its slender winding stems, is delicate, even fragile, yet this tough plant withstands the deepest snows and temperatures that can plummet to -49°F (-45°C).

ROSY LIGHTS
Rhododendron 'Rosy Lights'

The deep hues of the conch shell's mantle cannot best the warm tones of 'Rosy Lights' as its swollen buds expand to face the sun of May. This vigorous azalea adds a vibrancy to any shrub border when in bloom. Later its healthy green foliage can act as a foil for summer flowers, and in fall will turn a red as deep as fresh-cut cinnamon bark.

SPICY LIGHTS
Rhododendron 'Spicy Lights'

The blossoms of 'Spicy Lights' are a soft pastel of apricot and peach, colors rarely seen in hardy flowers. For those who desire fragrance, 'Spicy Lights' offers a perfume reminiscent of those same fruits, a perfume as sweet as Earth allows. This moderately vigorous, upright plant will grace your garden as few can, quickly becoming a treasured possession. Although probably too tender for sites in Zone 3, anyone living in warmer climes should try to find this delightful azalea.

WHITE LIGHTS
Rhododendron 'White Lights'

For sheer exuberance, 'White Lights' cannot be matched. Its upright stems erupt into a profusion of milk-white blossoms highlighted by a kiss of light pink. Even as a young plant, this hardy azalea puts on a floral display lasting several weeks. Although upright, 'White Lights' remains reasonably compact and dense, eventually forming a moderate-sized shrub, at home in any garden. Its foliage is plentiful, free of disease and a colorful yellow in the fall. It appears to be among the hardiest of the Northern Lights.

THE RHODODENDRONS

APRIL ROSE
Rhododendron 'April Rose'

This rhododendron has special meaning to me because its creator, Gustav Melquist of Connecticut, was my neighbor when I was a child. Decades later, in my new home, I came to realize what this modest man had accomplished in his lifetime, being a breeder of many important new plants. However, even if I had never known him, I would have included this variety, for it is a rhododendron of uncommon beauty and hardiness. The bush form is outstanding, being dense and compact. The small-leaved foliage is deep green with shadings of red-purple that become much deeper colored by fall. The double blossoms are a deep rose-lavender and are exceptionally prolific. It is an early bloomer, so be sure to locate it in a site that does not receive late spring frosts. Watching this beautiful plant grow in my garden has linked me with my old home in a most meaningful way. Few things in life have the ability to connect the past with the present as do garden plants. If you do not believe me, just keep gardening.

LAURIE
Rhododendron 'Laurie'

Rhododendrons of the past tended to be immense plants, more suited to large estates than to small urban gardens. Modern breeders have concentrated much of their efforts toward creating rhododendrons with compact habits. An excellent example of a successful hardy hybrid with this attribute is 'Laurie'. In five years this plant will probably grow no more than 20 in. (50 cm) tall and will be nearly as wide. Its generous crop of flowers is the most delicate of pinks, being nearly white from afar. The foliage is a somewhat mottled green and entirely clothes the branches, giving the plant great density. 'Laurie' has stood up against extremely low temperatures and strong winds, still opening up her buds in spring to grace the ground on which she grows.

OLGA MEZITT
Rhododendron 'Olga Mezitt'

This is one of many fine introductions by the Mezitt family of Weston Nurseries in Massachusetts. It is similar in many respects to the older 'PJM' hybrids but has *Rhododendron mucronulatum* as one of its parents rather than the *Rhododendron dauricum* of 'PJM'. 'Olga Mezitt' is a real color breakthrough. Most of the hardy hybrids were shades of lavender. 'Olga Mezitt' is a true pink. The foliage is healthy and easily tolerates Zone 4 winters. The winter foliage maintains its green color better than most of this group, having only a slight bronzy cast. This is a plant I have come to appreciate more as the years go by. It should not be confused with 'Aglo', its sister plant. 'Aglo' is a very beautiful variety with similar flowers but a deeper colored foliage. It is not as hardy as 'Olga Mezitt', although perfectly at home in Zone 5.

PJM
Rhododendron 'PJM'

Occasionally a plant appears that changes the face of gardening. The crossing of two rhododendron species, *Rhododendron dauricum* and *Rhododendron carolinianum*, by the Mezitt family of Weston Nurseries in Massachusetts resulted in a group of seedlings that had just such an impact. These hybrids were relatively compact plants with small glossy leaves that turned mahogany-red as winter arrived. In spring, masses of bloom transformed the plants into lavender cushions, but what set these plants apart from other notable rhododendrons was their hardiness. Within a

White Lights Azalea, *Rhododendron* 'White Lights' (p. 83)

Northern Hi-Lights Azalea, *Rhododendron* 'Northern Hi-Lights'

Laurie Rhododendron,
Rhododendron 'Laurie' (p. 84)

April Rose Rhododendron,
Rhododendron 'April Rose' (p. 83)

PJM Rhododendron, *Rhododendron* 'PJM' (p. 84)

Olga Mezitt Rhododendron, *Rhododendron* 'Olga Mezitt' (p. 84)

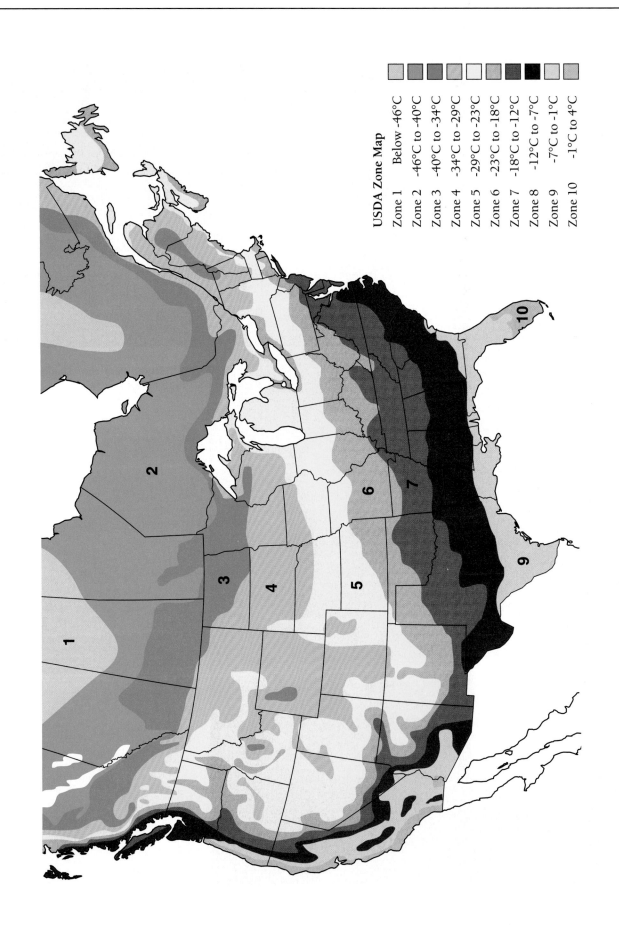

USDA Zone Map

Zone 1   Below -46°C
Zone 2   -46°C to -40°C
Zone 3   -40°C to -34°C
Zone 4   -34°C to -29°C
Zone 5   -29°C to -23°C
Zone 6   -23°C to -18°C
Zone 7   -18°C to -12°C
Zone 8   -12°C to -7°C
Zone 9   -7°C to -1°C
Zone 10   -1°C to 4°C

very short time, the 'PJM' rhododendron was being planted across North America, and in places where rhododendrons were considered only playthings for masochistic gardeners, the 'PJM' performed as no other rhododendron had. Now the 'PJM' is the most common rhododendron in northern gardens.

There were actually several seedlings raised in the breeding program, although they were very similar and were released under the umbrella name 'PJM', which stands for Peter J. Mezitt. These various clones are mixed up in the nursery trade now, although some nurseries do list them separately. The cultivars are 'Elite', 'Regal' and 'Victor'. 'Victor' is the first to bloom. 'Regal' blooms a day or two later, its color slightly darker. 'Elite' is last to bloom, making it the best choice for sites that get late spring frosts, for if the open flowers are hit by frost, they're done. Other cultivars of 'PJM' are offered by nurseries, but none are registered. It should be noted that 'PJM White', listed by some nurseries, is neither a 'PJM' cultivar, nor is it white. This cultivar is the result of crossing parents other than those of 'PJM'.

A hardy plant has to have a good record. As the years roll by, the 'PJM' continues to stand as the toughest of the tough. Individuals, by their interest and love, can transform a million gardens with their work and I give a nod of thanks to those who've spent their time so that we can see these wondrous sights. Luckily their work is not yet done, and many new wonders are waiting to be tested in gardens such as yours.

Appendix of Hardy Species

THE FOLLOWING IS A LIST OF TREE AND SHRUB SPECIES HARDY IN ZONE 5 or colder that are generally available in the nursery trade. Many more species exist that make excellent garden subjects but they can be difficult to locate. This appendix makes no attempt to cover all the characteristics of each species. Such an effort would require volumes. Rather it is a series of condensed descriptions outlining some of the ornamental characteristics that have made these species choices for gardens throughout the world.

Many forms and cultivated varieties selected from these species are used in horticulture. Often these varieties are grown for characteristics that set them apart from the normal species type. Others are outstanding representatives of the species.

Although a species may be listed as being hardy in cold areas, that same species may have a range that extends into much warmer climes. When growing trees or shrubs for cold-climate gardens, a responsible nursery will choose seed or cuttings from trees growing on the northern edge of the species' range. A tree grown from seed gathered in Alabama is unlikely to survive in Minnesota. Seek out nurseries that can tell you where their material originates. Being a successful gardener in the north depends to a great extent upon the origins of the material you plant.

KEY

LATIN NAME: The Latin name for a species is the same across the world. This universal system allows people to be sure they are talking about the same plant.

SPECIES COMMON NAME: Common names can vary from place to place. The common names given are those most often used to identify the species.

HARDINESS ZONE: Your garden lies within a hardiness zone that has been determined by the average minimum temperature. Although this is only one measure of a site's suitability for a given plant, it allows you to choose plants that are likely to survive your garden's winter temperatures. Consult the hardiness map to determine your zone. The colder the site, the lower the hardiness zone number. The zone number given for each species is the most northerly zone in which the species will grow without special protection.

AVERAGE MATURE HEIGHT: This figure represents the average height of a mature specimen in northern areas. An individual specimen may attain a greater or lesser height, but this will provide a basis for spacing your plants. Most references give the ultimate height, which is the height of the largest specimens growing under ideal conditions. The average height in the north will usually be noticeably lower than such figures. The seedlings of some species vary considerably in height. Such species are referred to as VH (variable height).

THE SPECIES

GENERALLY AVAILABLE TREES AND SHRUBS HARDY IN ZONE 5 AND COLDER

LATIN NAME	COMMON NAME	ZONE	AVG. HEIGHT
	FIR		
Abies alba	**EUROPEAN SILVER FIR**	4	100 ft. (30 m)
	A tall straight tree with horizontal branches. Needles are dark green and glossy with white bands on the undersides.		
Abies balsamea	**BALSAM FIR**	3	50 ft. (15 m)
	Straight conical tree with horizontal branches and gray bark with resin pockets, eventually scaly. Needles dark green with white bands on the undersides. Young cones are erect and purple, light brown when ripe.		
Abies concolor	**WHITE FIR**	4	100 ft. (30 m)
	Narrow upright tree with straight trunk and light gray rough bark. Thick blue-green needles. Several selections are available.		
Abies Fraseri	**FRASER FIR**	4	30 ft. (10 m)
	Small slender conical tree with short dark green needles. Young bark gray with resin blisters, turning scaly.		
Abies koreana	**KOREAN FIR**	5	50 ft. (15 m)
	Conical tree having dark green needles with white undersides. Deep purple cones.		
Abies lasiocarpa	**ALPINE FIR**	2	100 ft. (30 m)
	Tall, narrow conical to columnar tree with blue-green needles on upright branches. Purple cones.		
	MAPLE		
Acer dasycarpum	**SILVER MAPLE**	3	65 ft. (20 m)
	Large upright tree, often becoming quite wide in open sites. Leaves have 5 deeply notched lobes with whitish undersides. Often found in damp soils.		

LATIN NAME	COMMON NAME	ZONE	AVG. HEIGHT
	MAPLE		
Acer Ginnala	**AMUR MAPLE**	2	15 ft. (5 m)
	Small multi-stemmed tree with small 3-lobed leaves that turn deep red in fall.		
Acer Negundo	**BOX ELDER/MANITOBA MAPLE**	2	50 ft. (15 m)
	Rapid-growing tree usually with a short trunk and irregular branching. Leaves have 3-7 leaflets.		
Acer pensylvanicum	**STRIPED MAPLE**	3	40 ft. (12 m)
	Slender upright tree whose irregular branches gradually arch outward. Greenish bark with white stripes. Shade-tolerant species.		
Acer platanoides	**NORWAY MAPLE**	4	65 ft. (20 m)
	A large rounded tree with dark green leaves. Furrowed dark gray to black bark. Casts a dense shade. Yellow fall color.		
Acer rubrum	**RED MAPLE**	3	65 ft. (20 m)
	Upright, more spreading in the open. Flaky gray-brown bark. Flowers and fall color deep red. Often found in wet soils.		
Acer saccharum	**SUGAR MAPLE**	3	80 ft. (25 m)
	Upright tree with straight trunk that forms a wide oval shape in the open. Three-lobed leaves yellow-orange in fall. Prefers well-drained soils.		
	HORSE CHESTNUT		
Aesculus glabra	**OHIO BUCKEYE**	3	40 ft. (12 m)
	Rounded form with compound leaves and scaly bark. Nuts are encased in husks with short thorns. Tolerates clay soils.		
Aesculus Hippocastanum	**HORSE CHESTNUT**	5	65 ft. (20 m)
	Large rounded tree with compound leaves. Nut husks have sharp thorns. Tolerates clay soils.		
	ALDER		
Alnus crispa	**MOUNTAIN ALDER**	3	10 ft. (3 m)
	Multi-stemmed shrub that grows in wet sites as well as rocky slopes.		
Alnus glutinosa	**EUROPEAN BLACK ALDER**	4	40 ft. (12 m)
	Upright tree often found growing on damp soils.		
Alnus rugosa	**SPECKLED ALDER**	2	10 ft. (3 m)
	Vigorous, multi-stemmed upright to spreading shrub often found growing in old pasture land, particularly on damp soils. Nitrogen-fixing bacteria associate with the roots of alder.		
	SERVICEBERRY / JUNEBERRY		
Amelanchier alnifolia	**ALDERLEAF SERVICEBERRY**	2	15 ft. (5 m)
	Suckering upright shrub with white flowers in spring and edible red-purple fruit. Colorful fall foliage.		

LATIN NAME	COMMON NAME	ZONE	AVG. HEIGHT
	SERVICEBERRY / JUNEBERRY		
Amelanchier arborea	**DOWNY SERVICEBERRY**	3	30 ft. (10 m)
	Small slender tree with white flowers and edible red-purple fruit. Colorful fall foliage.		
Amelanchier canadensis	**OBLONGLEAF SERVICEBERRY**	3	40 ft. (12 m)
	Upright shrub or small tree with white flowers and edible blackish fruit. Colorful fall foliage.		
Amelanchier laevis	**SMOOTH SERVICEBERRY**	3	25 ft. (8 m)
	Upright shrub or small tree with white flowers and edible dark purple fruit. Colorful fall foliage.		
	BEARBERRY		
Arctostaphylos Uva-ursi	**EVERGREEN BEARBERRY**	3	7½ in. (.2 m)
	A trailing shrub with dark green shiny leaves. Small white or pink flowers followed by red berries.		
	CHOKEBERRY		
Aronia arbutifolia	**RED CHOKEBERRY**	2	10 ft. (3 m)
	A suckering shrub with white flowers in spring. Red fruit and foliage in fall.		
Aronia melanocarpa	**BLACK CHOKEBERRY**	2	6 ft. (2 m)
	A low shrub with white flowers in spring followed by black fruit. Red foliage in fall.		
	BARBERRY		
Berberis Thunbergii	**JAPANESE BARBERRY**	4	6 ft. (2 m)
	A dense shrub with sharp thorns, yellow flowers, small oval red fruit. Red-leaved forms are popular.		
	BIRCH		
Betula alleghaniensis	**YELLOW BIRCH/SILVER BIRCH**	3	65 ft. (20 m)
	Large tree with rounded top when grown in the open. Bark is silvery-yellow and peels off in thin strips.		
Betula mandschurica japonica	**JAPANESE WHITE BIRCH**	5	50 ft. (15 m)
	Upright tree with bright white bark.		
Betula nana	**DWARF BIRCH**	2	2½ ft. (.75 m)
	Small spreading shrub with small leaves.		
Betula nigra	**RIVER BIRCH/RED BIRCH**	4	80 ft. (25 m)
	A large tree with graceful branches. The bark is red-brown to silvery-gray when young, becoming rough with loose hanging sheets. Usually grows near streams and ponds where annual flooding occurs.		

LATIN NAME	COMMON NAME	ZONE	AVG. HEIGHT
	# BIRCH		
Betula papyrifera	**PAPER BIRCH/CANOE BIRCH**	2	80 ft. (25 m)
	A large tree with a relatively narrow crown and upright angled branches, sometimes more pendulous. Often grows in clumps. Snow-white bark that peels in thin sheets.		
Betula pendula	**EUROPEAN WHITE BIRCH**	3	50 ft. (15 m)
	A straight-trunked upright tree, usually with pendulous branches. Bark is white and peeling with dark rectangular flakes near the base. Many cultivated forms are available.		
Betula populifolia	**GRAY BIRCH**	2	25 ft. (8 m)
	A small narrow tree with white bark broken by dark scaly patches. Grows in acidic soil, often where poorly drained.		
	# PEA SHRUB		
Caragana arborescens	**CARAGANA/PEA SHRUB**	2	15 ft. (5 m)
	A vase-shaped multi-stemmed shrub with yellow-green shiny bark and compound leaves. Yellow flowers in late spring followed by small pods. Will grow in dry soils. Weeping forms are popular.		
Caragana frutex	**RUSSIAN PEA SHRUB**	2	10 ft. (3 m)
	Upright shrub with yellow spring flowers. The dwarfer form 'Globosa' is most commonly available.		
Caragana pygmaea	**PYGMY CARAGANA**	2	3 ft. (1 m)
	A dwarf upright shrub with bright yellow bark.		
	# HORNBEAM		
Carpinus caroliniana	**BLUE BEECH/IRONWOOD/ MUSCLEWOOD**	5	25 ft. (8 m)
	A small irregular tree with sinuous smooth gray bark. Usually grows near water.		
	# HACKBERRY		
Celtis occidentalis	**HACKBERRY/NETTLEBERRY/ SUGARBERRY**	3	100 ft. (30 m)
	A large upright tree with a narrow rounded crown and corky ridged bark.		
	# QUINCE		
Chaenomeles japonica	**LESSER FLOWERING QUINCE**	5	3 ft. (1 m)
	A small spreading shrub with orange blossoms in spring followed by small gnarled fruit. Spiny branches.		
Chaenomeles speciosa	**JAPANESE QUINCE/ FLOWERING QUINCE**	5	5 ft. (1.5 m)
	An upright to spreading shrub with spiny branches and red flowers in spring. Irregular apple-shaped fruit. Many cultivated forms.		

LATIN NAME	COMMON NAME	ZONE	AVG. HEIGHT
	FALSE CYPRESS		
Chamaecyparis obtusa	**HINOKI FALSE CYPRESS**	4-5	VH
	A large tree in its native Japan with flattened sprays of scaled needles. Many forms are too tender. Several dwarf forms are available, some of which are hardy.		
Chamaecyparis pisifera	**SAWARA CYPRESS**	4-5	VH
	Most forms are not hardy in the north but the 'Filifera' forms with their drooping thread-like foliage are hardy.		
	DOGWOOD		
Cornus alba	**TARTARIAN DOGWOOD**	2	10 ft. (3 m)
	A vigorous upright shrub that suckers outward. Red stems. There are many forms with various colored stems or leaves. Will grow in heavy or damp soils.		
Cornus alternifolia	**PAGODA DOGWOOD/ ALTERNATE-LEAVED DOGWOOD**	4	15 ft. (5 m)
	Small tree with horizontal branching pattern and yellow-green young stems. Flat round clusters of cream-white flowers followed by blue fruits.		
Cornus mas	**CORNELIAN CHERRY**	5	15 ft. (5 m)
	A small tree or large shrub with yellow flowers in early spring followed by dark red fruit. Several forms.		
Cornus racemosa	**GRAY DOGWOOD/ PANICLED DOGWOOD**	3	10 ft. (3 m)
	Large shrub with red fruits on gray branchlets. Narrow pointed leaves.		
Cornus sericea or *stolonifera*	**RED-OSIER DOGWOOD**	2	6 ft. (2 m)
	Spreading suckering shrub with deep red stems. White or pale blue fruit. Often found in damp sites such as roadside ditches. Several forms.		
	HAZELNUT		
Corylus americana	**AMERICAN HAZELNUT**	5	10 ft. (3 m)
	A multi-stemmed shrub with an edible nut encased in a long tubular covering.		
Corylus cornuta	**BEAKED HAZELNUT**	3	10 ft. (3 m)
	A multi-stemmed shrub with a small edible nut encased in a bristly tubular covering with a "beaked" tip.		
	COTONEASTER		
Cotoneaster acutifolius	**PEKING COTONEASTER**	3	10 ft. (3 m)
	A vase-shaped shrub with small shiny leaves and numerous small black fruits.		

LATIN NAME	COMMON NAME	ZONE	AVG. HEIGHT
	HAWTHORN		
Crataegus species	**HAWTHORN**	2-5	VH
	A complex group of related plants, usually multi-stemmed large shrubs, but sometimes single-stemmed and occasionally growing into small trees. White spring flowers and red fruit. Often has long sharp thorns. Tolerates poor drainage.		
	DAPHNE		
Daphne Cneorum	**ROSE DAPHNE/GARLAND FLOWER**	5	1 ft. (.3 m)
	A low evergreen shrub with extremely fragrant rose-pink blossoms in spring.		
Daphne Mezereum	**FEBRUARY DAPHNE**	4	3 ft. (1 m)
	A small erect shrub with fragrant purple flowers in very early spring. Red berries. Fruit and plant are poisonous. Short-lived, but renews itself with suckers.		
	ELAEAGNUS		
Elaeagnus angustifolia	**RUSSIAN OLIVE**	3	15 ft. (5 m)
	A small, usually multi-stemmed tree with sage-green leaves whose undersides are silvery. Fragrant flowers are followed by silvery fruits. Tolerates dry alkaline soils.		
Elaeagnus commutata	**SILVERBERRY**	2	10 ft. (3 m)
	Large shrub with silvery leaves, fragrant flowers and silvery fruit.		
	EUONYMUS		
Euonymus alata	**BURNING BUSH**	4	6-10 ft. (2-3 m)
	Shrub with dark green leaves and stems with corky wings. Small flowers are followed by small orange fruits. Brilliant red fall color. Several forms are in cultivation.		
Euonymus europaea	**EUROPEAN SPINDLE TREE**	4	15 ft. (5 m)
	Large shrub or small tree with red, pink or orange fruit clusters that hang down on long stems.		
	BEECH		
Fagus grandifolia	**AMERICAN BEECH**	3	80 ft. (25 m)
	Large tree with smooth gray bark and coarsely toothed leaves that turn yellow in autumn. Nuts are enclosed in a bristly husk. Being decimated by beech rust disease in northeastern forests.		

LATIN NAME	COMMON NAME	ZONE	AVG. HEIGHT

FORSYTHIA

Forsythia ovata	**KOREAN FORSYTHIA**	3	6 ft. (2 m)

A spreading shrub with dark green leaves and amber-yellow flowers in very early spring. New hardy hybrids of this species with larger flowers and deeper color have expanded ornamental forsythia growing into the north.

ASH

Fraxinus americana	**WHITE ASH**	4	100 ft. (30 m)

An upright narrow forest tree with a long straight trunk and tightly furrowed gray bark. In the open, white ash can become quite wide and spreading, often attaining a large thick trunk. Compound leaves. Often found growing near water. Tolerant of heavy soils.

Fraxinus excelsior	**EUROPEAN ASH**	4	100 ft. (30 m)

A large tree similar in many respects to white ash. There are many cultivated varieties.

Fraxinus nigra	**BLACK ASH**	3	65 ft. (20 m)

A narrow ash usually found on the edges of lakes or rivers. Wood was used for basketry.

Fraxinus pennsylvanica	**GREEN ASH/RED ASH**	3	50 ft. (15 m)

A narrow oval tree often found near water. Yellow fall color. Will grow in clay soils.

LOCUST

Gleditsia triacanthos	**HONEY LOCUST**	5	50 ft. (15 m)

A narrow, often crooked tree with large sharp thorns on the trunk and branches. Doubly compound leaves cast a dappled shade. Flowers are followed by long flat seed pods.

WITCH HAZEL

Hamamelis virginiana	**WITCH HAZEL**	4	6 ft. (2 m)

A multi-stemmed shrub with large oval leaves that turn yellow in fall. Small yellow flowers in late autumn.

HYDRANGEA

Hydrangea arborescens	**HILLS OF SNOW/ WILD HYDRANGEA**	4	5 ft. (1.5 m)

A spreading shrub with many upright stems. Large rounded white flower heads in late summer.

Hydrangea paniculata	**PEEGEE HYDRANGEA**	4	10 ft. (3 m)

A large shrub with large showy pyramidal flower heads, white turning pinkish, then brown.

LATIN NAME	COMMON NAME	ZONE	AVG. HEIGHT
HYDRANGEA			
Hydrangea quercifolia	**OAKLEAF HYDRANGEA**	5	6 ft. (2 m)
	A medium shrub with 5-lobed leaves. Large pyramidal flower heads, similar to Peegee hydrangea.		
HOLLY			
Ilex verticillata	**DECIDUOUS HOLLY/WINTERBERRY**	4	10 ft. (3 m)
	A multi-stemmed shrub with slightly glossy leaves, often having a purple cast. Small yellow flowers are followed by deep red berries close to the stems; berries persist into winter.		
WALNUT			
Juglans ailantifolia	**JAPANESE HEARTNUT**	4	50 ft. (15 m)
	Wide spreading tree with large compound leaves. The widely grown form is 'cordiformis', which has smooth shells that release the meats whole.		
Juglans cinerea	**BUTTERNUT**	3	65 ft. (20 m)
	Upright spreading tree with gray ridged bark and large compound leaves. Sharply ridged edible nuts are pointed and encased in a sticky covering that is used in dye making.		
Juglans nigra	**BLACK WALNUT**	5	80 ft. (25 m)
	Large upright and spreading tree with compound leaves. Edible nuts are round to oval, ridged and hard-shelled.		
JUNIPER			
Juniperus chinensis	**CHINESE JUNIPER**	4	VH
	An extremely diverse group of usually sharp-needled plants. Some grow as trees, others as low plants. Many cultivated forms.		
Juniperus communis	**COMMON JUNIPER**	3	VH
	Although there are tree forms, most grow as low spreading plants. Often found in groups on well-drained open land. Deep blue berries are used as flavoring for gin.		
Juniperus horizontalis	**CREEPING JUNIPER**	3	7½ in. (.2 m)
	A trailing plant that often forms large mats. Many cultivated forms.		
Juniperus procumbens	**JAPANESE GARDEN JUNIPER**	4	7½ in. (.2 m)
	A trailing plant with lime-green foliage. Often considered a variety of *J. chinensis*.		
Juniperus Sabina	**SAVIN JUNIPER**	3	VH
	Usually low-growing plants with slender needle-like foliage. Many cultivated forms.		
Juniperus scopulorum	**ROCKY MOUNTAIN JUNIPER**	4-5	20 ft. (6 m)
	A small to medium-sized tree with blue-green scaly needles.		

LATIN NAME	COMMON NAME	ZONE	AVG. HEIGHT
	JUNIPER		
Juniperus squamata	**SQUAMATA JUNIPER**	4	VH
	Usually a low-growing plant, sometimes higher. Usually found as cultivated forms.		
Juniperus virginiana	**RED CEDAR/PENCIL CEDAR**	5	15 ft. (5 m)
	Narrow upright tree, often pointed. Sharp-needled foliage often has a gray or bluish cast. Bark is red-brown and comes off in fine shreds. Wood and foliage are aromatic.		
	LAUREL		
Kalmia angustifolia	**SHEEP LAUREL/LAMBKILL/ DWARF LAUREL**	2	3 ft. (1 m)
	A dense low-growing evergreen shrub often found on poor, dry, acidic soils. Clusters of deep pink cupped flowers in early summer.		
Kalmia latifolia	**MOUNTAIN LAUREL**	5	6 ft. (2 m)
	A medium-sized evergreen shrub with dark green leathery leaves and clusters of pink cupped flowers in late spring/early summer. Many forms.		
	LARCH		
Larix decidua	**EUROPEAN LARCH**	3	100 ft. (30 m)
	A large, usually straight tree with horizontal branches that droop slightly but have upright tips. Fine needles turn yellow in fall.		
Larix Kaempferi	**JAPANESE LARCH**	5	80 ft. (25 m)
	A large tree with straight trunk and horizontal branching, sometimes pendulous. Foliage is fine and blue-green, turning yellow before dropping in fall.		
Larix laricina	**AMERICAN LARCH/TAMARACK/ HACKMATACK**	2	65 ft. (20 m)
	Usually a narrow upright tree, although open-grown specimens are sometimes irregular and wider. Usually straight-trunked with horizontal branching. Fine green needles turn yellow in fall.		
Larix sibirica	**SIBERIAN LARCH**	2	100 ft. (30 m)
	Narrow conical tree with upright branches that become horizontal with age. Young growth bright yellow, becoming green. Yellow fall foliage.		
	PRIVET		
Ligustrum amurense	**AMUR PRIVET**	5	10 ft. (3 m)
	Upright shrub with dark green glossy leaves. Often used for hedging. Several cultivars.		
Ligustrum vulgare	**COMMON PRIVET**	5	10 ft. (3 m)
	Glossy green leaves and dense habit make this shrub a popular choice for hedges.		

LATIN NAME	COMMON NAME	ZONE	AVG. HEIGHT
	HONEYSUCKLE		
Lonicera tatarica	**TATARIAN HONEYSUCKLE**	4	10 ft. (3 m)
	A narrow upright shrub with medium-green oval leaves and white, pink or red blossoms in late spring.		
Lonicera × xylosteoides	**DWARF HONEYSUCKLE**	3	8 ft. (2.5 m)
	A rounded dense shrub with lime-green soft leaves and pale yellow flowers in late spring. Superb hedging plant.		
	MAGNOLIA		
Magnolia acuminata	**CUCUMBER TREE**	5	80 ft. (25 m)
	A large tree with tightly furrowed bark and large oblong glossy leaves. Flowers appear with leaves and are yellow-green, fruit is cucumber-like, turning reddish.		
Magnolia × Loebneri	**LOEBNER MAGNOLIA**	5	13 ft. (4 m)
	A group of hybrids of *M. stellata* and *M. Kobus*. Trees are usually multi-stemmed and spreading with large white or pink flowers. Varieties vary in hardiness.		
Magnolia stellata	**STAR MAGNOLIA**	5	13 ft. (4 m)
	Usually a multi-stemmed small tree with oblong leaves and large star-like white flowers. Varieties vary in hardiness.		
	APPLE		
Malus baccata	**SIBERIAN CRAB**	2	13 ft. (4 m)
	A small tree or shrub with white flowers followed by yellow fruit flushed red. The hardiest apple.		
Malus floribunda	**SHOWY CRAB**	5	20 ft. (6 m)
	A rounded small tree with arched branches and reddish twigs. Rosy blooms in spring followed by yellow fruit.		
Malus hupehensis	**TEA CRAB**	5	20 ft. (6 m)
	A spreading tree with stiff branches. White to pink flowers followed by small yellow-red fruits.		
Malus × Niedzwetzkyana	**ROSYBLOOM CRABS**	3	23 ft. (7 m)
	Hybrids using hardy species crossed with this cultivar of *M. pumila* have various shades of pink and red flowers. These are treated as a group in horticulture.		
Malus prunifolia	**PLUM-LEAFED APPLE/ CHINESE APPLE**	4	25 ft. (8 m)
	A small to medium-sized tree with white flowers followed by persistent yellow or red fruits.		
Malus pumila	**COMMON APPLE**	4	30 ft. (10 m)
	A medium-sized tree, usually upright when young, becoming more spreading and often pendulous with age. White or pink flowers are followed by yellow or red fruits. The source of most edible apples.		

LATIN NAME	COMMON NAME	ZONE	AVG. HEIGHT
	APPLE		
Malus Sargentii	**SARGENT'S CRAB**	4	6 ft. (2 m)
	A small spreading tree with white blossoms and small deep red fruit.		
Malus Sieboldii	**TORINGO CRAB**	5	10 ft. (3 m)
	A small tree with arching branches. Flowers are bright pink, fading to white, fruit small, red and persistent.		
Malus spectabilis	**CHINESE FLOWERING APPLE**	5	15 ft. (5 m)
	Large spreading shrub or small tree with bright pink blossoms and small yellow fruit.		
	BAYBERRY		
Myrica pensylvanica	**BAYBERRY/CANDLEBERRY**	5	6 ft. (2 m)
	A dense, partially evergreen shrub found growing on poor sandy soils and seashores. Fruit has a waxy coating used to make bayberry candles.		
	HOP HORNBEAM		
Ostrya virginiana	**HOP HORNBEAM/IRONWOOD**	4	30 ft. (10 m)
	A slow-growing sinuous tree often found in the forest understory. Flaking gray or brown bark. Extremely dense wood used in making handles.		
	CLIFF-GREEN		
Paxistima Canbyi	**MOUNTAIN-LOVER/RATSTRIPPER**	4	7½ in. (.2 m)
	An evergreen spreading ground cover with small oblong glossy leaves.		
	AMUR CORKTREE		
Phellodendron amurense	**AMUR CORKTREE**	4	50 ft. (15 m)
	A medium to large tree with relatively narrow crown, sometimes spreading with age. Thick corky bark and shiny compound leaves.		
	MOCK ORANGE		
Philadelphus species	**MOCK ORANGE**	4	VH
	There are many mock oranges available in horticulture, many of which are hybrids of several species. Most grow into upright shrubs with fragrant white blossoms. Many cultivated forms.		
	NINEBARK		
Physocarpus opulifolius	**NINEBARK**	3	10 ft. (3 m)
	Vigorous shrub with exfoliating bark and small pink flowers in early summer. Several varieties have yellowish foliage.		
	SPRUCE		
Picea Abies	**NORWAY SPRUCE**	3	80 ft. (25 m)
	Tall conical evergreen with drooping branches and hanging branchlets. An immense number of cultivars are grown.		

LATIN NAME	COMMON NAME	ZONE	AVG. HEIGHT
	SPRUCE		
Picea Engelmannii	**ENGELMANN SPRUCE**	3	80 ft. (25 m)
	A dense wide conical tree with bluish-green needles. Branches are horizontal to slightly ascending.		
Picea glauca	**WHITE SPRUCE**	3	65 ft. (20 m)
	A large conical evergreen with horizontal branching and dark green, sometimes bluish, foliage.		
Picea mariana	**BLACK SPRUCE**	2	50 ft. (15 m)
	Usually a very narrow straight tree with thin pendulous branches. Often found in poorly drained or swampy ground.		
Picea Omorika	**SERBIAN SPRUCE**	4	80 ft. (25 m)
	Tall, very narrow evergreen with drooping branches that sweep upward at the tips. Characteristic white bands on undersides of needles. Deep purple cones are produced even on young trees.		
Picea pungens	**COLORADO SPRUCE**	3	100 ft. (30 m)
	Tall narrow evergreen with blue-green foliage. Needles are long and sharp. Many selections, mostly deep blue, are available.		
Picea rubens	**RED SPRUCE**	2	100 ft. (30 m)
	Large conical spruce with reddish-brown scaly bark on a straight trunk. Needles are yellow-green and shiny.		
	PINE		
Pinus albicaulis	**WHITE-BARK PINE**	4	30 ft. (10 m)
	Sometimes found growing as an upright tree, but often more shrubby. White peeling bark.		
Pinus aristata	**BRISTLECONE PINE**	4	30 ft. (10 m)
	Very slow-growing pine, sometimes upright but more often irregular. White resin dots on densely crowded needles.		
Pinus Banksiana	**JACK PINE**	2	80 ft. (25 m)
	Sometimes tall and upright but more often an irregular shrubby tree with an open branching habit. Stiff, twisted dark green needles.		
Pinus Bungeana	**LACEBARK PINE**	5	65 ft. (20 m)
	Upright but often shrubby pine with peeling white bark as it ages.		
Pinus Cembra	**SWISS STONE PINE**	3	30 ft. (10 m)
	Slow-growing upright, usually narrow tree with long needles.		
Pinus contorta	**LODGEPOLE PINE/SHORE PINE/ BEACH PINE**	4	30 ft. (10 m)
	Variable in habit, usually short and rounded, but can be narrow with long stemless trunks when growing in groves. Short twisted dark green needles.		
Pinus koraiensis	**KOREAN PINE**	5	65 ft. (20 m)
	Relatively narrow conical habit. Slow growing. Source of edible pine nuts.		

LATIN NAME	COMMON NAME	ZONE	AVG. HEIGHT
	PINE		
Pinus Mugo	**MUGO PINE**	2	13 ft. (4 m)
	Usually a wide shrubby pine, but occasionally growing as a small tree. The *pumila* form is low and wide. Many forms available. *P. uncinata* is similar but grows as a tall tree.		
Pinus nigra	**AUSTRIAN PINE**	4	100 ft. (30 m)
	Large, wide, dense pine with long dark green needles. Usually branched to the base.		
Pinus resinosa	**NORWAY PINE/RED PINE**	3	80 ft. (25 m)
	A large straight tree with horizontal branching. In groups it forms a long, straight branchless trunk used for poles. Long dark green needles.		
Pinus rigida	**PITCH PINE**	5	50 ft. (15 m)
	Open, irregular, often with tufts of short branches. Needles are stiff and twisted. Resinous wood.		
Pinus Strobus	**WHITE PINE**	3	100 ft. (30 m)
	A large open tree with horizontal branching. Needles are long and soft, usually blue-green in color. Used for timber and cultivated in many forms.		
Pinus sylvestris	**SCOTS PINE**	3	65 ft. (20 m)
	Sometimes straight growing, more often slightly irregular with open habit. Stiff needles are often blue-green in color. A variable species depending on site and seed source. Several varieties are cultivated.		
Pinus Thunbergiana	**JAPANESE BLACK PINE**	5	100 ft. (30 m)
	A large tree, sometimes growing with irregular habit. Branches horizontal to slightly pendulous. Used extensively for shore plantings.		
Pinus virginiana	**VIRGINIA PINE/SCRUB PINE**	4	30 ft. (10 m)
	A shrub form of pine with stiff twisted needles. Grows on poor soils.		
	POPLAR		
Populus alba	**WHITE POPLAR/ SILVER-LEAFED POPLAR**	4	65 ft. (20 m)
	A rounded tree, often multi-stemmed with 3-5 lobed leaves, glossy green above and white underneath, giving the tree a silvery appearance. Suckers readily.		
Populus balsamifera	**BALSAM POPLAR**	2	100 ft. (30 m)
	Fast-growing upright tree with sticky winter buds. Usually available as the sterile hybrid 'Balm-of-Gilead'.		
Populus × canadensis	**CAROLINA POPLAR**	4	100 ft. (30 m)
	A hybrid tree that is extremely fast growing. Will form a large tree with a very large diameter trunk.		
Populus canescens	**GRAY POPLAR**	3	30 ft. (10 m)
	Tall growing whose foliage has grayish undersides. Most notable as a parent of 'Tower' poplar.		

LATIN NAME	COMMON NAME	ZONE	AVG. HEIGHT
	POPLAR		
Populus deltoides	**COTTONWOOD**	2	80 ft. (25 m)
	A large wide tree when open-grown. Large glossy green leaves. Fast growing. Often found in river-bottom soils.		
Populus nigra	**BLACK POPLAR**	3	80 ft. (25 m)
	Usually found as the tall narrow form known as 'Lombardy'. Very fast growing and short-lived in northern areas. Several new forms have been bred using this species as a parent.		
Populus tremula	**EUROPEAN ASPEN**	2	80 ft. (25 m)
	Large wide tree sometimes used in breeding work.		
Populus tremuloides	**TREMBLING ASPEN**	1	80 ft. (25 m)
	An extremely hardy species usually found in large groves. Leaves are attached to the stems by a thin petiole, allowing the leaves to tremble in the slightest breeze. Yellow fall color.		
	CINQUEFOIL		
Potentilla fruticosa	**POTENTILLA/ SHRUBBY CINQUEFOIL**	2	4 ft. (1.2 m)
	A dense low shrub with numerous yellow, white or orange blossoms from early summer to frost. Many cultivars are available.		
Potentilla parvifolia	**POTENTILLA/ SHRUBBY CINQUEFOIL**	2	3 ft. (1 m)
	Similar to *P. fruticosa* but having finer foliage. Yellow flowers.		
	PLUM/CHERRY		
Prunus Maackii	**MAYDAY CHERRY**	2	30 ft. (10 m)
	A large rounded tree with hanging clusters of white flowers, followed by small black fruit.		
Prunus maritima	**BEACH PLUM/SHORE PLUM**	4	6 ft. (2 m)
	A sprawling shrub native to the shores of northeastern America. White flowers followed by small edible but tart purple or yellow fruit.		
Prunus Padus	**BIRD CHERRY**	4	30 ft. (10 m)
	One of the larger cherry trees. Shiny reddish-brown peeling bark. Hanging clusters of white bloom followed by black astringent fruit.		
Prunus pensylvanica	**PIN CHERRY/BIRD CHERRY**	2	25 ft. (8 m)
	Upright to slightly spreading, small and short-lived tree with shiny red-brown bark, white flowers and bright red acidic fruit. Common on disturbed or burned areas.		
Prunus serotina	**BLACK CHERRY/RUM CHERRY**	4	65 ft. (20 m)
	A large tree, often with a sizable trunk. Bark becomes black and segmented. White flowers in spring followed by red to black fruit. Important source of furniture wood.		

LATIN NAME	COMMON NAME	ZONE	AVG. HEIGHT
	PLUM/CHERRY		
Prunus tomentosa	**NANKING CHERRY/ CHINESE BUSH CHERRY**	3	8 ft. (2.5 m)
	A dense rounded shrub with slightly hairy textured foliage and pink blossoms in early spring. Bright red cherries are juicy and edible.		
Prunus triloba	**FLOWERING ALMOND**	4	6 ft. (2 m)
	Available as a cultivated shrub with double pink blossoms. Does not set fruit. Flowers in early spring.		
Prunus virginiana	**CHOKECHERRY**	2	13 ft. (4 m)
	An upright suckering small tree with hanging clusters of white blossoms in early spring and red to black astringent fruit.		
	DOUGLAS FIR		
Pseudotsuga Menziesii	**DOUGLAS FIR**	4	80 ft. (25 m)
	Although most Douglas fir will not survive in the colder regions, some seed sources will produce hardy trees. A narrow upright tree with light green needles. Grows immense in its natural range.		
	PEAR		
Pyrus communis	**COMMON PEAR**	4	30 ft. (10 m)
	Narrow and upright when young but becoming spreading or pendulous as it ages. Glossy green foliage and white blossoms in early spring. The source of edible pears.		
Pyrus ussuriensis	**SIBERIAN PEAR**	3	65 ft. (20 m)
	A large upright, sometimes spreading tree with glossy foliage and clouds of white blossoms in early spring. Produces green, hard astringent fruit.		
	OAK		
Quercus alba	**WHITE OAK**	5	80 ft. (25 m)
	Large spreading tree, often attaining immense stature in southern areas. Northern seed sources are important for hardiness. Leathery round-lobed leaves turning brown in fall and often persisting into winter.		
Quercus coccinea	**SCARLET OAK**	4	65 ft. (20 m)
	Medium-sized oak with deeply lobed dark green leaves that turn a brilliant scarlet in fall. Most often found on dry soils.		
Quercus imbricaria	**SHINGLE OAK**	5	50 ft. (15 m)
	Generally a medium-sized upright tree, but sometimes irregular. Leaves are dark green and elliptical with no lobes.		
Quercus macrocarpa	**BUR OAK/MOSSYCUP OAK**	3	80 ft. (25 m)
	Often a large tree with somewhat sinuous and twisting branches, often become more rounded with age and with downturned lower limbs. Round-lobed leaves occur in many different patterns but usually have one deep indentation on each side.		

LATIN NAME	COMMON NAME	ZONE	AVG. HEIGHT
	## OAK		
Quercus palustris	**PIN OAK**	4	65 ft. (20 m)
	Open-grown specimens form remarkably precise pyramidal cones whose branches grow slightly downward. Leaves turn red in fall and often persist into winter.		
Quercus robur	**ENGLISH OAK**	5	65 ft. (20 m)
	A large upright oak, growing wide in open sites. Leaves have rounded lobes and persist into winter. Several cultivars are grown.		
Quercus rubra	**RED OAK**	4	80 ft. (25 m)
	A large tree with dark furrowed bark and leaves with sharply pointed lobes. Foliage is a dusky red in fall and often persists into winter.		
	## RHODODENDRON/AZALEA		
Rhododendron sp.	**RHODODENDRON/AZALEA**	4	VH
	A large group of plants, only a few of which are hardy in colder sites. The rhododendrons are evergreen while the azaleas lose their leaves in winter. Spectacular flowers of various colors in spring or early summer. Generally found growing in moist acidic soils. Habits vary considerably from compact to loose, short to tall.		
	## SUMAC		
Rhus aromatica	**FRAGRANT SUMAC/LEMON SUMAC**	4	6 ft. (2 m)
	A shrub with compound aromatic leaves and clusters of yellow flowers that produce hairy red fruit.		
Rhus glabra	**SMOOTH SUMAC/SCARLET SUMAC**	4	15 ft. (5 m)
	A shrub with smooth, slightly flattened stems, compound leaves and short clusters of hairy red fruit.		
Rhus typhina	**STAGHORN SUMAC**	3	15 ft. (5 m)
	This upright coarsely stemmed plant has soft furry stems and compound leaves that turn yellow, orange and red in fall. Yellow flowers produce upright pyramidal clusters of hairy red fruit.		
	## CURRANT		
Ribes alpinum	**ALPINE CURRANT**	2	8 ft. (2.5 m)
	A vigorous dense shrub with medium green foliage. Popular hedging plant.		
Ribes aureum	**GOLDEN CURRANT**	2	6 ft. (2 m)
	A vigorous arching shrub that spreads by runners. Yellow flowers in late spring are powerfully fragrant and reminiscent of cloves.		
	## BLACK LOCUST		
Robinia Pseudoacacia	**BLACK LOCUST/FALSE ACACIA**	4	65 ft. (20 m)
	An upright tree with a short trunk and picturesquely irregular branches. Long, fragrant hanging flower clusters produce short flat seed pods. Very attractive to honey bees.		

LATIN NAME	COMMON NAME	ZONE	AVG. HEIGHT
	## ROSE		
Rosa × alba	**ALBA ROSE**	4	6 ft. (2 m)
	A group of roses probably derived from a cross between *R. canina* and *R. damascena*. Flowers are generally white or pink with a loose form. Usually highly fragrant. A number of cultivars are available.		
Rosa canina	**DOG ROSE/BRIER ROSE**	4	10 ft. (3 m)
	Vigorous arching shrub with hooked thorns and pink or white single blooms. Has been used extensively in the breeding of many named varieties. Commonly used as a rootstock for budded roses.		
Rosa carolina	**PASTURE ROSE**	4	3 ft. (1 m)
	A low suckering shrub with reddish stems. Pink single roses in late spring.		
Rosa centifolia	**CABBAGE ROSE**	5	5 ft (1.5 m)
	A suckering shrub with numerous thorny stems bearing nodding pink flowers. Many cultivated varieties. Usually fragrant.		
Rosa foetida	**AUSTRIAN BRIER ROSE**	3	6 ft. (2 m)
	Coarse upright shrub with slender prickly canes. Flowers have unusual fragrance. Commonly available hybrids are yellow and yellow-orange.		
Rosa gallica	**FRENCH ROSE**	4	5 ft. (1.5 m)
	Moderately vigorous shrub with bristly canes and fragrant pink or red flowers. Many cultivated varieties are available.		
Rosa multiflora	**MULTIFLORA ROSE**	4	6 ft. (2 m)
	A vigorous dense plant most commonly used as a rootstock for rose varieties. Arching green or red canes have numerous hooked thorns, although some are thornless. Single small white or pale pink blooms. Used for hybridization.		
Rosa nitida	**NITIDA ROSE**	3	2½ ft. (.75 m)
	A low suckering shrub with numerous fine thorns. Flowers usually pink with strong fragrance. Dark red hips. Select varieties have semi-double blooms.		
Rosa pendulina	**ALPINE ROSE**	3	6 ft. (2 m)
	Tall arching shrub with smooth or lightly thorned stems. Single pink flowers in spring followed by bright red vase-shaped hips.		
Rosa rugosa	**RUGOSA ROSE/JAPANESE ROSE**	2	6 ft. (2 m)
	A suckering shrub with numerous thorns and single white, pink or red fragrant flowers in late spring or early summer. Used extensively for breeding. Many cultivated varieties, often having repeat blooming and double flowers.		
Rosa spinosissima	**SCOTCH ROSE/BURNET ROSE**	3	5 ft. (1.5 m)
	A dense suckering shrub with slender, well-armed stems. Flowers occur in spring and are usually white or light pink. Many cultivars have been bred using this species. Usually very fragrant.		

LATIN NAME	COMMON NAME	ZONE	AVG. HEIGHT
	## WILLOW		
Salix alba	**WHITE WILLOW**	2	30 ft. (10 m)
	Upright densely branched tree. Young stems are usually yellow, occasionally reddish. Long slender leaves with whitish undersides. Several selected varieties are available, including weeping types. Often found on damp soils.		
Salix caprea	**PUSSY WILLOW**	4	20 ft. (6 m)
	An upright shrub with smooth stems and soft gray catkins that appear in early spring before the leaves. Usually found in damp ground.		
	## ELDERBERRY		
Sambucus canadensis	**AMERICAN ELDER**	4	8 ft. (2.5 m)
	An upright coarse suckering shrub with stiff hollow stems. White umbrella-shaped flower clusters occur in early summer, followed by purple-black berries that are used in cooking and wine making.		
Sambucus pubens	**RED ELDER/STINKING ELDER**	4	8 ft. (2.5 m)
	A coarse vase-shaped shrub with loose clusters of white flowers in early spring followed by inedible red berries.		
	## MOUNTAIN ASH		
Sorbus americana	**AMERICAN MOUNTAIN ASH**	2	25 ft. (8 m)
	A small tree, usually multi-stemmed and vase-shaped. Brown smooth bark becoming somewhat broken in old age. Compound leaves. Flat clusters of white flowers in spring turn into small deep red fruits.		
Sorbus Aucuparia	**EUROPEAN MOUNTAIN ASH/ROWAN**	2	50 ft. (15 m)
	An upright tree with an oval crown. Compound leaves. Flat clusters of white flowers followed by orange to red fruit.		
Sorbus decora	**SHOWY MOUNTAIN ASH/ NORTHERN MOUNTAIN ASH**	2	25 ft. (8 m)
	Similar in most respects to *S. americana* but with shorter leaflets and larger deep red fruit.		
Sorbus reducta	**DWARF MOUNTAIN ASH**	5	3 ft. (1 m)
	A very dwarf multi-stemmed shrub with compound leaves.		
	## SPIREA		
Spiraea japonica	**JAPANESE SPIREA**	4	3 ft. (1 m)
	Although the wild species can form sizable shrubs, many cultivated varieties form dense small shrubs with fine branching and small leaves. Small pink or white flowers on terminals in early summer.		
Spiraea nipponica	**TOSA SPIREA**	4	6 ft. (2 m)
	Smooth arching branches and small rounded leaves with small flowers in globular clusters in early summer. Cultivated varieties are often more compact.		

LATIN NAME	COMMON NAME	ZONE	AVG. HEIGHT
	## SPIREA		
Spiraea trilobata	**THREE-LOBED SPIREA**	4	3 ft. (1 m)
	A spreading plant with smooth wiry stems and small blue-green leaves. White flowers in small flat clusters appear in early summer.		
Spiraea × Vanhouttei	**BRIDAL-WREATH SPIREA**	3	6 ft. (2 m)
	A graceful arching shrub with small leaves. Pure white blossoms in small clusters along the stems blossom in late spring.		
	## SNOWBERRY		
Symphoricarpos albus	**SNOWBERRY/WAXBERRY**	3	3 ft. (1 m)
	A suckering small shrub often forming large thickets. Small pink flowers form white berries that hang on into winter if not eaten by birds. Will grow in very damp soil.		
Symphoricarpos × Chenaultii	**CORALBERRY**	4	3 ft. (1 m)
	A suckering small shrub with spiked flowers that form purple-red fruits.		
Symphoricarpos occidentalis	**WOLFBERRY**	3	5 ft. (1.5 m)
	A dense arching and mounding shrub with gray-green leaves, light pink blossoms and white fruit.		
Symphoricarpos orbiculatus	**CORALBERRY/INDIAN CURRANT**	3	6 ft. (2 m)
	A suckering shrub with small pink flowers that form coral-red fruits.		
	## LILAC		
Syringa × chinensis	**CHINESE LILAC**	3	13 ft. (4 m)
	A large upright shrub with slightly pendulous clusters of fragrant lilac blossoms in late spring. Several cultivated varieties are available.		
Syringa × hyacinthiflora	**HYACINTH LILAC**	3	15 ft. (5 m)
	A hybrid between *S. oblata* and *S. vulgaris* that forms a large upright shrub with stout branches and loose clusters of lightly fragrant flowers in late spring. Flowers after common lilac. Several colors available.		
Syringa Meyeri	**MEYER'S LILAC**	4	5 ft. (1.5 m)
	A small and slow-growing shrub with clusters of lavender-pink bloom in late spring. The cultivar 'Palibin' is virtually the only available form.		
Syringa microphylla	**LITTLELEAF LILAC**	4	8 ft. (2.5 m)
	A slow-growing wide shrub with long thin branches that droop when in flower. The pale pink flowers are in showy groups of smaller clusters.		
Syringa oblata	**EARLY BLOOMING LILAC/ BROADLEAF LILAC**	4	8 ft.(2.5 m)
	Upright to spreading shrub with large thick leaves that turn maroon in fall. Clusters of lilac blossoms in early spring.		

LATIN NAME	COMMON NAME	ZONE	AVG. HEIGHT
	## LILAC		
Syringa patula	**KOREAN LILAC/DWARF LILAC**	4	6 ft. (2 m)
	A small and slow-growing shrub that is relatively dense and refined in form. Pale lavender blooms have a spicy fragrance. Variety most commonly grown is 'Miss Kim'.		
Syringa pekinensis	**PEKING LILAC**	4	13 ft. (4 m)
	A small tree, often shrubby with red-brown bark that peels off in papery flakes. Flowers in late spring are pale yellow with a honey fragrance.		
Syringa persica	**PERSIAN LILAC**	4	6 ft. (2 m)
	A medium-sized shrub with slender arching branches and clusters of fragrant lilac-pink blooms in late spring.		
Syringa × prestoniae	**PRESTON LILACS**	2	13 ft. (4 m)
	Hybrids between *S. villosa* and *S. reflexa* that form vigorous shrubs with large, loose pyramidal clusters of fragrant bloom in late spring. Many cultivated varieties are available.		
Syringa reticula	**JAPANESE TREE LILAC**	3	25 ft. (8 m)
	A moderate-sized tree, usually multi-stemmed with shiny cherry-like bark and large loose pyramidal clusters of fragrant creamy-white blossoms in late spring or early summer.		
Syringa villosa	**LATE LILAC**	2	10 ft. (3 m)
	A large shrub with pyramidal clusters of light pink or lilac blooms in late spring or early summer.		
Syringa vulgaris	**COMMON LILAC**	2	13 ft. (4 m)
	A large suckering shrub with tight clusters of highly fragrant blooms in spring. A widely distributed species with hundreds of varieties available.		
	## ARBORVITAE/EASTERN WHITE CEDAR		
Thuja occidentalis	**WHITE CEDAR/ARBORVITAE**	3	80 ft. (25 m)
	A dense oval or pyramidal tree with aromatic foliage. Generally found in wet soils or on limestone soils. Many cultivars are available in a wide range of shapes and textures.		
	## LINDEN/BASSWOOD		
Tilia americana	**AMERICAN LINDEN/BASSWOOD**	3	100 ft. (30 m)
	A large broad tree, usually with a straight thick trunk. Large heart-shaped leaves and fragrant blossoms in summer that are attractive to bees. Wood is favorite carving material.		
Tilia cordata	**LITTLELEAF LINDEN**	3	80 ft. (25 m)
	A medium to large tree with small heart-shaped leaves. Fragrant blossoms in summer are attractive to bees. Many cultivars available.		
Tilia platyphyllos	**LARGE-LEAVED LINDEN**	4	100 ft. (30 m)
	A large tree having large heart-shaped leaves with soft-textured undersides.		
Tilia tomentosa	**SILVER LINDEN/WHITE LINDEN**	4	80 ft. (25 m)
	A broad pyramidal tree. Large leaves have silvery undersides.		

LATIN NAME	COMMON NAME	ZONE	AVG. HEIGHT
	HEMLOCK		
Tsuga canadensis	**CANADIAN HEMLOCK**	3	80 ft. (25 m)
	Often forming a large irregular pyramidal tree with small, flat, deep green needles and a loose feathery appearance. Often found growing in cool moist soils. Will grow in shaded conditions.		
Tsuga caroliniana	**CAROLINA HEMLOCK**	5	65 ft. (20 m)
	Similar in most respects to the Canadian hemlock but with slightly longer needles and cones.		
	ELM		
Ulmus americana	**AMERICAN ELM**	3	100 ft. (30 m)
	A large vase-shaped arching tree with furrowed dark bark. Once extensively planted as a street tree but now decimated by Dutch elm disease.		
Ulmus glabra	**SCOTCH ELM/WYCH ELM**	5	30 ft. (10 m)
	A wide spreading tree with large textured leaves. The weeping form 'Camperdownii' is the only commonly available cultivar.		
Ulmus pumila	**SIBERIAN ELM**	3	30 ft. (10 m)
	A small dense tree, sometimes shrubby but often trained to a single stem with small dark green leaves.		
	BLUEBERRY		
Vaccinium angustifolium	**LOWBUSH BLUEBERRY**	2	11 in. (.3 m)
	A low suckering shrub with small glossy leaves. White to pinkish flowers form deep blue edible fruit by late summer. Often brilliant red fall color. Grows in well-drained acidic soil.		
Vaccinium corymbosum	**HIGHBUSH BLUEBERRY**	4	8 ft. (2.5 m)
	Upright shrub with white or pink flowers that form large edible blue fruit. Grows in acidic soils.		
Vaccinium macrocarpon	**AMERICAN CRANBERRY**	2	7½ in. (.2 m)
	A mat-like shrub growing to 3 ft.(1 m) across. Small glossy green leaves. Clusters of small pink flowers form deep red fruit used commercially. Grows in acidic bogs and swamps.		
Vaccinium Vitis-idaea	**LINGONBERRY/FOXBERRY**	4	7½ in. (.2 m)
	A creeping evergreen plant with small leathery foliage and pink or white blossoms that form small red sour but edible fruit.		
	VIBURNUM		
Viburnum alnifolium	**HOBBLEBUSH/MOOSEWOOD**	4	10 ft. (3 m)
	A coarse shrub with very large textured leaves. In late spring, a large grouping of smaller fertile flowers surrounded by a ring of large white sterile flowers appears, followed by purple-black fruits. Foliage turns red in fall. Shade tolerant.		

LATIN NAME	COMMON NAME	ZONE	AVG. HEIGHT
	VIBURNUM		
Viburnum cassinoides	**WILD RAISIN/WITHE-ROD/ APPALACHIAN TEA**	4	10 ft. (3 m)
	Upright shrub with lance-shaped glossy green leaves. White round clusters in early summer. Fruits are blue-black.		
Viburnum dentatum	**ARROWWOOD**	3	13 ft. (4 m)
	A variable species. Usually stems and undersides of leaves are hairy but not always. Round clusters of white flowers form blue-black fruits.		
Viburnum Lantana	**WAYFARING TREE**	3	13 ft. (4 m)
	Upright, often rounded shrub with large, textured, fuzzy leaves. Flowers come in round clusters and are white. Fruit is red, turning black. Will tolerate shady conditions.		
Viburnum Lentago	**NANNYBERRY/SHEEPBERRY**	3	25 ft. (8 m)
	A large upright shrub or small tree with pointed egg-shaped leaves and round, textured stems. White flowers in late spring form blue-black fruits.		
Viburnum Opulus	**EUROPEAN CRANBERRY**	3	10 ft. (3 m)
	A coarse upright to rounded shrub with a rounded cluster of fertile flowers surrounded by a ring of larger white sterile flowers. Fruit is juicy and red. Used for jellies. Several cultivated varieties, some with only large sterile flowers.		
Viburnum plicatum	**JAPANESE SNOWBALL**	5	10 ft. (3 m)
	Horizontally layered shrub with white clusters of flowers that form red, then black fruits. Some cultivars have large clusters of sterile flowers.		
Viburnum prunifolium	**SWEET HAW/BLACK HAW**	3	13 ft. (4 m)
	Shrub with round white flower clusters followed by black fruit, which can be eaten after frost.		
Viburnum trilobum	**HIGHBUSH CRANBERRY**	2	13 ft. (4 m)
	Coarse shrub similar in nearly every respect to V. *Opulus*. White flower clusters followed by edible but sour red fruit.		
	WEIGELA		
Weigela species	**WEIGELA/CARDINAL FLOWER**	4	VH
	A variable group of many-branched shrubs derived from several species, often being hybrids between species. Flowers are usually pink or red shades. Blossoms are tubular and attract hummingbirds.		

Index

Abbotswood (potentilla), 70
Acer Ginnala, 36
Acer pensylvanicum, 37
Acer rubrum, 37-38
Acer saccharum, 37
acidity (soil), 6, 7
Aglo (rhododendron), 84
Agnes (rose), 72
alder, 88
alkalinity (soil), 6
Amelanchier species, 38
American larch, 52-53, 95
American linden, 45, 106
American mountain ash, 45
ammonium nitrate, 11
Amur corktree, 97
Amur maple, 36, 88
annual rye grass, 12
ants, 33
aphids, 30
apple scab, 42
apple trees, 41-43, 96-97
April Rose (rhododendron), 83-84
arborvitae (cedar), 60-64, 106
Arcadia (juniper), 51
ash, 39-30, 45, 93, 104
auxins, 19, 23
azalea, 81-83, 102

bacteria, 9, 10-11
bacterial infections, 32
barberrry, 89
bark, shredded, 13, 14
basswood, 45, 106
bayberry, 97
bearberry, 89
beech, 92
beetles, 34-35
birch, 89-90
black locust (tree), 102
Blanc Double de Coubert (rose), 72
blister beetle, 34-35
bloodmeal, 10, 12, 14
Blue Danube (juniper), 51
blue spruce, 57-59
blueberry, 77, 107
bonemeal, 16
bonsai, 26, 50
borers, 35

botanical names, xi, 42, 86
    list of, 87-108
Brandon (cedar), 61
bridal-wreath spirea, 73-74, 105
bristlecone pine, 59
broadleaf evergreens, 80-85
buckwheat, 12
bur oak, 44, 101
burning bush, 66-67
butternut, 40-41, 94

calcium, 5, 6
calcium nitrate, 11
Calgary Carpet (juniper), 49-50
cambium, 18, 35
Canadian hemlock, 64-65
candleberry, 97
canker, 24, 31-32, 45
carbon, 7, 10
carbon dioxide, 7, 8, 11, 18
carbon:nitrogen ratio, 10, 11
caterpillars, 34
cedar, 60-64
cells, 1, 17-18
cherry (tree), 100-01
Chinese lilac, 76
chlorophyll, 7, 18
chloroplasts, 18
chokeberry, 89
cinquefoil, 100
clay–humus complex, 6, 7, 13
clay soils, 5, 7, 13, 14, 15
cliff-green, 80-81, 97
Cole's Prostrate (hemlock), 64-65
Colorado spruce, 57-59, 98
common lilac, 76, 106
compost, 10-11, 12, 13, 15, 16
conifers, 48-65
cotoneaster, 91
cottonseed meal, 12
couchgrass, 12, 13
crabapple, 41-43, 96-97
crabmeal, 12
cranberry, 107
Crataegus mordenensis 'Toba', 38-39
crown gall, 27
cultivation, 13-14
    as cause of stress, 29
currant (shrub), 102

cutleaf sumac, 46
cypress, 91

daphne (shrub), 92
deciduous holly, 68, 94
deciduous trees, 36-47
    pruning, 22-25
    weak crotches, 23-24
decomposition, 8, 9-10, 13
    See also compost; nitrogen
diseases
    apple scab, 42
    bacterial infections, 32
    canker, 24, 31-32, 45
    crown gall, 27
    Dutch elm disease, 24, 35
    fireblight, 24, 32, 42, 45
    fungal infection, 23, 24
    Juglans dieback, 24, 40-41
    mildew, 31, 42
    milky spore disease, 34
    preventing, 17, 29-30
    rust, 32
    treating, 31-32
    viruses, 32
    See also plants, under stress
dogwood, 91
Douglas fir, 101
drainage, 13
drought stress, 14
Dutch elm disease, 24, 35
dwarf Alberta spruce, 55-56
dwarf blue spruce, 58-59
dwarf Korean lilac, 76, 106
dwarf Serbian spruce, 56-57, 98

eastern hemlock, 64-65
eastern white cedar, 60-64, 106
elaeagnus, 92
elderberrry, 104
elevation (garden site), 2
elm, 107
    disease, 24, 35
elm bark beetle, 35
Emerald (cedar) 63
ethylene, 19
euonymus, 92
Euonymus alata, 66-67
evergreens, 48-65

broadleaf, 80-85
pruning, 25-26

false cypress, 91
fertilizers
chemical, 11
compost, 10-11, 12, 13, 15, 16
granular, 17
green manure, 12
manure, 10, 12
negative consequences of use, 29
nitrogen, 8-19, 16
organic, 7
fireblight, 24, 32, 42, 45
firs, 87
fishmeal, 10, 12, 14
Floppy Disc (potentilla), 70
flowering crabapple, 41-43
flowering shrubs/bushes, 66-79
pruning, 20-22
forsythia, 20, 67-68, 93
Forsythia ovata, 67
Forsythia × ovata 'Northern Gold',
67-68
Fraxinus americana, 39-40
Fraxinus pennsylvanica, 40
fruit-bearing trees, 25, 41-43, 100-01
fruits
mildew, 31
and pruning, 22
fungal growth, 28-29
fungal infection, 23, 24

garden
as ecosystem, 30
mulches, 13-14
proximity to buildings, 2
site, selecting, 1-3
temperatures in, 2
in winter, 69
Golden Globe (cedar), 61
Golden Lights (azalea), 82-83
Goldfinger (potentilla), 70
Goldflame (spirea), 74
Goldmount (spirea), 74
green ash, 40
green manure, 12
growth hormones, 19
gypsy moth, 34

hackberry, 90
hackmatack, 52-53, 95

hardy species, list of, 86-108
hardiness zone, defined, 86-87
hawthorn, 38-39, 92
hazelnut, 91
"heading back" (technique), 19, 20
hemlock, 64-65, 107
highbush blueberry, 77, 107
hoeing, 13
holly, 68, 94
honeysuckle, 96
Holmstrup (cedar), 62
hop hornbeam, 97
hornbeam, 90
horse chestnut, 88
humus, 5, 7, 13
hydrangea, 93-94

ice formation, 29
Ilex verticillata, 68
insecticidal soap, 33, 34
insecticides, 30, 34
insects, 28-31
aphids, 30, 33
beetles, 34-35
borers, 35
caterpillars, 34
controlling, 33-35
leaf miners, 34
natural enemies of, 30, 33
scale insects, 33
Iseli Fastigiata (spruce), 58

Japanese beetle, 34
Japanese garden juniper, 50, 94
Japanese tree lilac, 47, 106
Jeddeloh (hemlock), 65
Jens Munk (rose), 72
Juglans cinerea, 40-41
Juglans dieback, 24, 40-41
juneberry, 38, 88-89
juniper, 48-52, 94-95
Juniperus communis 'Suecica', 51-52
Juniperus horizontalis, 48
Juniperus horizontalis 'Douglasii', 50
Juniperus horizontalis 'Yukon Belle', 50
Juniperus procumbens 'Nana', 50
Juniperus Sabina, 48
Juniperus Sabina 'Arcadia', 51
Juniperus Sabina 'Blue Danube', 51
Juniperus scopolorum 'Wichita Blue', 52
Juniperus species, 48-52
Juniperus × media 'Mint Julep', 51

Königin Von Dänemark (rose), 72
Korean forsythia, 67, 68, 93

ladybugs, 33
larch, 52-53, 95
Larix laricina, 52
Latin names, list of, 87-108
laurel, 95
Laurie (rhododendron), 84
layering (mulches), 13, 14
leaf miners, 34
leaves
absorption of water, 28
aphids, 33
beetles, 34-35
caterpillars, 34
cells, 18
fungal growth on, 28-29
leaf miners, 34
mildew, 31
rust, 32
legumes, 8, 12
lilac, 74-76, 105-06
lime, 6, 7, 10, 13
linden, 45, 106
linseed meal, 12
Little Champion (cedar), 62
Little Gem (cedar), 62
Little Gem (spruce), 54
Little Giant (cedar), 62
littleleaf linden, 45
Little Princess (spirea), 74
locust (tree), 93
loess soils, 5
Lombardy poplar, 43, 100
lowbush blueberry, 77

magnesium, 5, 6
magnolia, 41, 96
Magnolia stellata 'Royal Star', 41
Malus Niedzwetzkyana
(red-veined crab), 42-43
Malus species, 41-43
manure, 10, 12
See also green manure
maple trees, 36-38, 87-88
meatmeal, 12
Melquist, Gustav, 83-84
Merrill magnolia, 41
mildew, 31, 42
milky spore disease, 34
minerals, 5-6, 7-8
Minima (hemlock), 65

Mint Julep (juniper), 51
Minuet (weigela), 79
mock orange, 68, 97
mossycup oak, 44, 101
mountain ash, 104
mountain-lover, 80-81, 97
Mugo pine, 59-60, 99
mulching, 13-14, 30
mycorrhizae, 30

nest spruce, 53-54
Nigra (cedar), 62-63
ninebark, 69, 97
nitrogen, 8-10
    in composting, 10-11
    in garden mulches, 14
    soluble forms of, 11
    sources of, 8-9, 12
    and transplants (roots), 16
northern gold forsythia, 67-68
Norway spruce, 53-55, 97
nutrients
    absorption of, 17, 18
    in compost, 10-11
    organic matter, 7, 8-9, 10, 11
    plant growth, 7
    in soil, 7-10
nut trees, 40-41, 88, 94

oak, 44, 101-02
Ohlendorff (spruce), 54
Olga Mezitt (rhododendron), 84
Orchid Lights (azalea), 83
organic matter
    breakdown of, 10, 11
    compost, 10-11
    decomposition of, 9-10, 11
    providing nutrients, 7, 8-12
    sources of, 10, 13
overwatering, 12
oxygen, 7, 9, 10, 12, 13, 14, 18

pea shrub, 90
pear trees, 101
peat moss, 14, 15
perennial rye grass, 12
pest control, 30, 33-35
pesticides, 29, 30, 34
pests, 30, 33-35
pH (potential hydrogen) level, 6, 10
pheremones, 30
Philadelphus × virginalis, 68

phloem, 18
phosphorus, 16
photosynthesis, 7, 30
Physocarpus opulifolius, 69
Picea Abies, 53
Picea Abies 'Farnsburg', 55
Picea Abies 'Little Gem', 54
Picea Abies 'Nidiformis', 53-54
Picea Abies 'Ohlendorfii', 54
Picea glauca, 55
Picea glauca albertiana 'Conica', 55-56
Picea Omorika, 56
Picea Omorika 'Nana', 56-57
Picea pungens, 57
Picea pungens 'Iseli Fastigiata', 58
Picea pungens 'Thomsen', 58
Picea pungens 'Thume', 58-59
pinching terminals, 21
pine, 25-26, 59-60, 98-99
Pinus aristata, 59
Pinus Mugo, 59-60
PJM (rhododendron), 84-85
planting, 2, 14-17
planting hole, 14-15, 16
plants
    choosing, 22, 29
    cytology of, 7-8, 17-18
    decomposition, 8
    green colour of, 18
    and growth cycle, 1
    ideal soil, 5
    and nutrient cycle, 7-8
    rootbound, 16
    strategic placement of, 2-3
    transplanting (potted), 14-17, 29
    under stress, 12, 14, 18
        defenses against being, 28
        during winter, 2, 29
plum tree, 100-01
poplar, 43-44, 99-100
Populus canescens 'Tower', 43-44
potassium, 5
potentilla, 69-70, 100
Potentilla fruticosa, 69-70
Potentilla fruticosa 'Abbotswood', 70
Potentilla fruticosa 'Floppy Disc', 70
Potentilla fruticosa 'Goldfinger', 70
Potentilla fruticosa 'Primrose Beauty', 71
Potentilla fruticosa 'Red Ace', 71
potting soils, 14-15
Preston hybrids (lilac), 76, 106
Primrose Beauty (potentilla), 71
privet, 95

proteins, 8
pruning
    negative consequences of,
        18, 27, 29
    purpose of, 17
    roots, 26-27
    shrubs, 19-22
    techniques, 20-22, 25, 27
    tools, 27-28
    trees
        deciduous, 22-25
        evergreen, 25-26
    wounds, 23, 26, 31
pussywillow, 104

Quadra (rose), 72
Quercus macrocarpa, 44
Quercus rubra, 44
quince, 90

ratstripper, 80-81, 97
Red Ace (potentilla), 71
Red Jade, 42
Red Maple, 37-38, 88
Red Oak, 44
Red Prince (weigela), 79
rhododendron, 81-82, 83-85, 102
Rhododenron 'April Rose', 83-84
Rhododendron carolinianum, 84
Rhododendron dauricum, 84
Rhododendron 'Golden Lights', 82
Rhododendron 'Laurie', 84
Rhododendron mucronulatum, 84
Rhododendron 'Olga Mezitt', 84
Rhododendron 'Orchid Lights', 83
Rhododendron 'PJM', 84-85
Rhododendron 'Rosy Lights', 83
Rhododendron species, 81
Rhododendron 'Spicy Lights', 83
Rhododendron 'White Lights', 83
Rhus typhina, 46
Rhus typhina 'Laciniata', 46
Rocky Mountain juniper, 52, 94
roots
    absorption of water, 17, 18
    before planting, 16
    crown gall, 27
    direction of growth, 14, 18
    dwarf root, 25
    fertilizing, 16
    mulches, 14
    and organic matter, 9, 12
    pruning, 18, 26-27

Rosa 'Agnes', 72
Rosa alba, 72
Rosa 'Blanc Double de Coubert', 72
Rosa 'Jens Munk', 72
Rosa 'Königin Von Dänemark', 72
Rosa 'Quadra', 72
Rosa rugosa, 72
Rosa species, 71
Rosa 'Stanwell Perpetual', 73
Rosa 'Thérèse Bugnet', 73
Rosa 'William Baffin', 73
roses
    pruning, 20
    rust, 32
    shrubs/bushes, 71-73, 103
Rosy Lights (azalea), 83
royal star magnolia, 41
Rudolph (crabapple), 42-43
rust, 32

sandy soils, 5, 7, 8
sap, 4, 17, 18, 37
    bleeding, 24
Sargent, Charles S., 65
Sargent's Weeping (hemlock), 65
scale insects, 33
Seagreen (juniper), 51
seeds, 1, 21-22
Selkirk (crabapple), 43
Serbian spruce, 56-57, 98
serviceberry, 38, 88-89
shearing
    shrubs, 20
    trees, 23, 25-26
shrubs
    absorption of water/nutrients,
        17, 18
    and alkaline soil, 6-7
    average mature height(s), 87-108
    diseases, 31-32
    flowering, 66-79
    growth hormones, 19
    planting, 2-3, 14-17
    preferred pH level, 6
    pruning, 19-22, 27
    stress
        defenses against, 28
        winter, 29
    in Zone 5 (and colder), 87-108
silica, 5, 8
silt, 5, 7
silver linden, 45
site, selecting, 1-3

Skinner, Frank Leith, 43
Smaragd (cedar), 63
snowberry, 105
Snowbird Hawthorn, 38
sodium, 5
soil, 3-12
    acidity, 6, 7
    alkalinity, 6, 7
    clay, 5-6, 7, 14
    components of, 5
    crumbly, 5
    cultivating, 13-14
    density, 14
    drainage, 13
    in dry climates, 6-7
    low-nitrogen, 9
    minerals in, 5-6, 7-8
    organic material in, 8-10
    providing nutrients, 7-8, 9, 11-12
    rocks in, 8, 14
    sandy, 7
    supplements, 10-12
    tests, 6
    texture, 5-7, 14
Sorbus americana, 45
southwest injury, 2
soybean meal, 12
Spicy Lights (azalea), 83
Spiraea Bumalda 'Goldflame', 74
Spiraea Bumalda 'Goldmound', 74
Spiraea japonica 'Little Princess', 74
Spiraea species, 73-74
Spiraea × Vanhouttei, 73-74
spirea, 73-74, 104-05
spring pruning, 20, 24
spruce, 53-59, 97-98
Staghorn sumac, 46
Stanwell Perpetual (rose), 73
stomata, 7, 18
striped maple, 37, 88
sugar maple, 37, 88
sulfur, 7
sumac, 46, 102
summer pruning, 20, 25, 27
Sunkist (cedar), 63
sunlight, 7, 18, 30
supercooling, 29
Swedish juniper, 51-52
Syringa × chinensis, 7
Syringa × prestoniae, 76
Syringa reticula, 47
Syringa species, 74
Syringa vulgaris, 76

tamarack, 52-53, 95
Tango (weigela), 79
temperature
    compost pile, 10
    hardiness zone(s), 86-108
    and mulched gardens, 14
    and pH levels, 6
    during winter, 2, 29
tent caterpillar, 34
Thérèse Bugnet (rose), 73
thinning, 20, 23, 26
Thomsen (spruce), 58
Thuja occidentalis 'Brandon', 61
Thuja occidentalis 'Golden Globe', 61
Thuja occidentalis 'Holmstruppi', 62
Thuja occidentalis 'Little Champion', 62
Thuja occidentalis 'Little Gem', 62
Thuja occidentalis 'Little Giant', 62
Thuja occidentalis 'Nigra', 62-63
Thuja occidentalis 'Smaragd', 63
Thuja occidentalis 'Sunkist', 63
Thuja occidentalis 'Unicorn', 63
Thuja occidentalis 'Woodwardii', 63-64
Thume (spruce), 58-59
Tilia americana, 45
Tilia cordata, 45
Toba Hawthorn, 48-49
tools
    cultivation, 13
    pruning, 27-28
Tower Poplar, 43-44
transpiration, 17
transplanting, 14-17
    and root pruning, 26-27
    and stress to plant, 29
trees
    absorption of water/nutrients,
        17, 18
    and alkaline soil, 6-7
    average mature height(s), 87-108
    broadleaf evergreens, 80-85
    conifers, 48-65
    deciduous, 37-47
    diseases in, 31-32
    formation of branches/leaves, 18
    fruit-bearing, 25, 41-43, 100-01
    growth hormones, 19, 23
    growth rings, 18
    nut, 40-41, 88, 94
    planting, 2-3, 14-17
    preferred pH level, 6
    pruning, 22-26
    staking, 17

under stress, 23-24, 33, 35
   defenses against being, 28
   winter, 29
  in Zone 5 (and colder), 87-108
Tsuga canadensis, 64
Tsuga canadensis 'Cole's Prostrate', 64-65
Tsuga canadensis 'Jeddeloh', 65
Tsuga canadensis 'Minima', 65
Tsuga canadensis 'Sargentii', 65
Tsuga heterophylla, 64

urea, 11

Vaccinium angustifolium, 77
Vaccinium corymbosum, 77
vetch, 13
viburnum, 77, 107-08
Vibernum cassinoides, 78
Vibernum Lantana, 78
Vibernum species, 77
virginal mock orange, 68

viruses, 32

walnut, 94
water
  absorption of, 17
   and root pruning, 26
  and compost pile, 10, 11
  and light potting mix, 14-15
  loss of in leaves, 17
  moving through soil, particles, 5
  and mulch gardening, 14
  and plant growth, 7-8, 12, 14
  roots before planting, 14-15
  in soil, 3, 5, 6-7, 12
Waukegan, 50
wayfaring tree, 78, 108
web worms, 34
weed control, 13-14
weeping Norway spruce, 55
weigela, 78-79, 108
Weigela 'Red Prince', 79

Weigela species, 78-79
Weigela 'Tango', 79
western hemlock, 64
white ash, 39-40, 93
White Lights (azalea), 83
white spruce, 55-56
Wichita Blue (juniper), 52
wild raisin, 78, 108
William Baffin (rose), 73
willow, 104
windchill, 2
winter survival, 2, 29
winterberry, 68, 94
witch hazel, 93
Woodwardii, 63-64

xylem, 17-18

Yukon Belle, 50

Zone 5, hardy species (list), 86-108